HANNAH ARENDT

HANNAH ARENDT
THE LAST INTERVIEW
and OTHER CONVERSATIONS

 MELVILLE HOUSE
BROOKLYN · LONDON

HANNAH ARENDT: THE LAST INTERVIEW
AND OTHER CONVERSATIONS

First Melville House printing: December 2013

Melville House Publishing   8 Blackstock Mews
145 Plymouth Street   and   Islington
Brooklyn, NY 11201   London N4 2BT

mhpbooks.com   facebook.com/mhpbooks   @melvillehouse

Library of Congress Cataloging-in-Publication Data

Arendt, Hannah, 1906-1975.
    Hannah Arendt : the last interview and other conversations /
Hannah Arendt.
        pages cm
    ISBN 978-1-61219-311-3 (pbk.)
    ISBN 978-1-61219-312-0 (ebk)
    1. Arendt, Hannah, 1906-1975–Interviews.   2. Arendt,
Hannah 1906-1975–Political and social views.   3. Political
science–Philosophy.   I. Title.

JC251.A74A5 2013
320.5092–dc23
                                                2013037680

Printed in the United States of America
3   5   7   9   10   8   6   4   2

CONTENTS

"WHAT REMAINS? THE LANGUAGE REMAINS":

A CONVERSATION WITH GÜNTER GAUS

ZUR PERSON, ZDF TV, GERMANY
OCTOBER 28, 1964

TRANSLATED BY JOAN STAMBAUGH

On October 28, 1964, the following conversation between Hannah Arendt and Günter Gaus, at the time a well-known journalist and later a high official in Willy Brandt's government, was broadcast on West German television. The interview was awarded the Adolf Grimme Prize and was published the following year under the title "Was bleibt? Es bleibt die Muttersprache" in Günter Gaus, *Zur Person*, Munich, 1965. This English translation is by Joan Stambaugh and it first appeared in *Essays on Understanding*, edited by Jerome Kohn (Harcourt Brace Jovanovich, 1994).

Gaus begins the conversation by saying that Arendt is the first woman to take part in the series of interviews he is conducting; then he immediately qualifies that statement by noting that she has a "very masculine occupation," namely, that of philosopher. This leads him to his first question: In spite of the recognition and respect she has received, does she perceive "her role in the circle of philosophers" as unusual or peculiar because she is a woman? Arendt replies:

ARENDT: I am afraid I have to protest. I do not belong to the circle of philosophers. My profession, if one can even speak of it at all, is political theory. I neither feel like a philosopher, nor do I believe that I have been accepted in the circle of philosophers, as you so kindly suppose. But to speak of the other question that you raised in your opening remarks: you say that philosophy is generally thought to be a masculine

3

occupation. It does not have to remain a masculine occupation! It is entirely possible that a woman will one day be a philosopher ...*

GAUS: I consider you to be a philosopher ...

ARENDT: Well, I can't help that, but in my opinion I am not. In my opinion I have said good-bye to philosophy once and for all. As you know, I studied philosophy, but that does not mean that I stayed with it.

GAUS: I should like to hear from you more precisely what the difference is between political philosophy and your work as a professor of political theory.

ARENDT: The expression "political philosophy," which I avoid, is extremely burdened by tradition. When I talk about these things, academically or nonacademically, I always mention that there is a vital tension between philosophy and politics. That is, between man as a thinking being and man as an acting being, there is a tension that does not exist in natural philosophy, for example. Like everyone else, the philosopher can be objective with regard to nature, and when he says what he thinks about it he speaks in the name of all mankind. But he cannot be objective or neutral with regard to politics. Not since Plato!

---

* The ellipses here and elsewhere are in the original; they do not indicate omission of material.

GAUS: I understand what you mean.

ARENDT: There is a kind of enmity against all politics in most philosophers, with very few exceptions. Kant *is* an exception. This enmity is extremely important for the whole problem, because it is not a personal question. It lies in the nature of the subject itself.

GAUS: You want no part in this enmity against politics because you believe that it would interfere with your work?

ARENDT: "I want no part in this enmity," that's it exactly! I want to look at politics, so to speak, with eyes unclouded by philosophy.

GAUS: I understand. Now, let us turn to the question of women's emancipation. Has this been a problem for you?

ARENDT: Yes, of course; there is always the problem as such. I have actually been rather old-fashioned. I have always thought that there are certain occupations that are improper for women, that do not become them, if I may put it that way. It just doesn't look good when a woman gives orders. She should try not to get into such a situation if she wants to remain feminine. Whether I am right about this or not I do not know. I myself have always lived in accordance with this more or less unconsciously—or let us rather say, more or less consciously. The problem itself played no role for me personally. To put it very simply, I have always done what I liked to do.

GAUS: Your work—we will surely go into details later—is to a significant degree concerned with the knowledge of the conditions under which political action and behavior come about. Do you want to achieve extensive influence with these works, or do you believe that such influence is no longer possible in these times, or is it simply not important to you?

ARENDT: You know, that is not a simple question. If I am to speak very honestly I would have to say: When I am working, I am not interested in how my work might affect people.

GAUS: And when you are finished?

ARENDT: Then I am finished. What is important for me is to understand. For me, writing is a matter of seeking this understanding, part of the process of understanding ... Certain things get formulated. If I had a good enough memory to really retain everything that I think, I doubt very much that I would have written anything—I know my own laziness. What is important to me is the thought process itself. As long as I have succeeded in thinking something through, I am personally quite satisfied. If I then succeed in expressing my thought process adequately in writing, that satisfies me also.

You ask about the effects of my work on others. If I may wax ironical, that is a masculine question. Men always want to be terribly influential, but I see that as somewhat external. Do I imagine myself being influential? No. I want to understand. And if others understand—in the same sense that I have understood—that gives me a sense of satisfaction, like feeling at home.

GAUS: Do you write easily? Do you formulate ideas easily?

ARENDT: Sometimes I do; sometimes I don't. But in general I can tell you that I never write until I can, so to speak, take dictation from myself.

GAUS: Until you have already thought it out.

ARENDT: Yes. I know exactly what I want to write. I do not write until I do. Usually I write it all down only once. And that goes relatively quickly, since it really depends only on how fast I type.

GAUS: Your interest in political theory, in political action and behavior, is at the center of your work today. In this light, what I found in your correspondence with Professor Scholem* seems particularly interesting. There you wrote, if I may quote you, that you were "interested in [your] youth neither in politics nor in history." Miss Arendt, as a Jew you emigrated from Germany in 1933. You were then twenty-six years old. Is your interest in politics—the cessation of your indifference to politics and history—connected to these events?

ARENDT: Yes, of course. Indifference was no longer possible in 1933. It was no longer possible even before that.

* Gershom Scholem (1897–1982), German-born Zionist, historian, and eminent scholar of Jewish mysticism, was an old acquaintance of Hannah Arendt's. On June 23, 1963, he wrote a highly critical letter to her about her book *Eichmann in Jerusalem*; see *"Eichmann in Jerusalem*: An Exchange of Letters," *Encounter* 22 (1964). The quotation given here is from Arendt's reply, dated July 24, 1963.

GAUS: For you as well?

ARENDT: Yes, of course. I read the newspapers intently. I had opinions. I did not belong to a party, nor did I have need to. By 1931 I was firmly convinced that the Nazis would take the helm. I was always arguing with other people about it but I did not really concern myself systematically with these things until I emigrated.

GAUS: I have another question about what you just said. If you were convinced that the Nazis could not be stopped from taking power, didn't you feel impelled actively to do something to prevent this—for example, join a party—or did you no longer think that made sense?

ARENDT: I personally did not think it made sense. If I had thought so—it is very difficult to say all this in retrospect— perhaps I would have done something. I thought it was hopeless.

GAUS: Is there a definite event in your memory that dates your turn to the political?

ARENDT: I would say February 27, 1933, the burning of the Reichstag, and the illegal arrests that followed during the same night. The so-called protective custody. As you know, people were taken to Gestapo cellars or to concentration camps. What happened then was monstrous, but it has now been overshadowed by things that happened later. This was an immediate shock for me, and from that moment on I felt responsible. That is, I was no longer of the opinion that one can simply be a bystander. I tried to help in many ways. But what actually took me out of Germany—if I should speak of that; I've never told it because it is of no consequence—

GAUS: Please tell us.

ARENDT: I intended to emigrate anyhow. I thought immediately that Jews could not stay. I did not intend to run around Germany as a second-class citizen, so to speak, in whatever form. In addition, I thought that things would just get worse and worse. Nevertheless, in the end I did not leave in such a peaceful way. And I must say that gives me a certain satisfaction. I was arrested, and had to leave the country illegally—I will tell you how in a minute—and that was instant gratification for me. I thought at least I had done something! At least I am not "innocent." No one could say that of me!

The Zionist organization gave me the chance. I was close friends with some of the leading people, above all with the then president, Kurt Blumenfeld. But I was not a Zionist. Nor did the Zionists try to convert me. Yet in a certain sense I was influenced by them: especially by the criticism, the self-criticism that the Zionists spread among the Jewish people. I was influenced and impressed by it, but politically I had nothing to do with Zionism. Now, in 1933 Blumenfeld and someone whom you do not know approached me and said: We want to put together a collection of all anti-Semitic statements made in ordinary circumstances. For example, statements in clubs, all kinds of professional clubs, all kinds of professional journals—in short, the sort of thing that doesn't become known in foreign countries. To organize such a collection at that time was to engage in what the Nazis called "horror propaganda." No Zionist could do this, because if he were found out, the whole organization would be exposed . . . They asked me, "Will you do it?" I said, "Of course." I was very happy. First of all, it seemed a very intelligent idea to me, and second, it gave me the feeling that something could be done after all.

GAUS: Were you arrested in connection with this work?

ARENDT: Yes. I was found out. I was very lucky. I got out after eight days because I made friends with the official who arrested me. He was a charming fellow! He'd been promoted from the criminal police to a political division. He had no idea what to do. What was he supposed to do? He kept saying to me, "Ordinarily I have someone there in front of me, and I just check the file, and I know what's going on. But what shall I do with you?"

GAUS: That was in Berlin?

ARENDT: That was in Berlin. Unfortunately, I had to lie to him. I couldn't let the organization be exposed. I told him tall tales, and he kept saying, "I got you in here. I shall get you out again. Don't get a lawyer! Jews don't have any money now. Save your money!" Meanwhile the organization had gotten me a lawyer. Through members, of course. And I sent this lawyer away. Because this man who arrested me had such an open, decent face. I relied on him and thought that here was a much better chance than with some lawyer who himself was afraid.

GAUS: And you got out and could leave Germany?

ARENDT: I got out, but had to cross the border illegally ... my name had not been cleared.

GAUS: In the correspondence we mentioned, Miss Arendt, you clearly rejected as superfluous Scholem's warning that you should always be mindful of your solidarity with the Jewish people. You wrote—I quote again: "To be a Jew belongs for me to the indubitable facts of my life, and I never wanted to change anything about such facts, not even in my childhood." I'd like to ask a few questions about this. You were born in 1906 in Hannover as the daughter of an engineer, and grew up in Königsberg. Do you remember what it was like for a child in prewar Germany to come from a Jewish family?

ARENDT: I couldn't answer that question truthfully for everyone. As for my personal recollection, I did not know from my family that I was Jewish. My mother was completely a-religious.

GAUS: Your father died young.

ARENDT: My father had died young. It all sounds very odd. My grandfather was the president of the liberal Jewish community and a civil official of Königsberg. I come from an old Königsberg family. Nevertheless, the word "Jew" never came up when I was a small child. I first met up with it through anti-Semitic remarks—they are not worth repeating—from children on the street. After that I was, so to speak, "enlightened."

GAUS: Was that a shock for you?

ARENDT: No.

GAUS: Did you have the feeling, Now I am something special?

ARENDT: That is a different matter. It wasn't a shock for me at all. I thought to myself: That is how it is. Did I have the feeling that I was something special? Yes! But I could no longer unravel that for you today.

GAUS: In what way did you feel special?

ARENDT: Objectively, I am of the opinion that it was related to being Jewish. For example, as a child—a somewhat older child then—I knew that I looked Jewish. I looked different from other children. I was very conscious of that. But not in a way that made me feel inferior; that was just how it was. Then, too, my mother, my family home, so to speak, was a bit different from the usual. There was so much that was special about it, even in comparison with the homes of other Jewish children or even of other children who were related to us, that it was hard for a child to figure out just what was special.

GAUS: I would like some elucidation as to what was special about your family home. You said that your mother never deemed it necessary to explain your solidarity with Jewishness to you until you met up with it on the street. Had your mother lost the sense of being Jewish which you claim for yourself in your letter to Scholem? Didn't it play a role for her any more at all? Was she successfully assimilated, or did she at least believe so?

ARENDT: My mother was not a very theoretical person. I do not believe that she had any special ideas about this. She herself came out of the Social Democratic movement, out of the circle of the *Sozialistische Monatshefte*,* as did my father. The question did not play a role for her. Of course she was a Jew. She would never have baptized me! I think she would have boxed my ears right and left if she had ever found out that I had denied being a Jew. It was unthinkable, so to speak. Out of the question! But the question was naturally much more important in the twenties, when I was young, than it was for my mother. And when I was grown up it was much more important for my mother than in her earlier life. But that was due to external circumstances. ╱

I myself, for example, don't believe that I have ever considered myself a German—in the sense of belonging to the people as opposed to being a citizen, if I may make that distinction. I remember discussing this with Jaspers around 1930. He said, "Of course you are German!" I said, "One can see that I am not!" But that didn't bother me. I didn't feel that it was something inferior. That wasn't the case at all. And to

* *Sozialistische Monatshefte* (*Socialist Monthly*) was a well-known German journal of the time.

come back once again to what was special about my family home: all Jewish children encountered anti-Semitism. And it poisoned the souls of many children. The difference with us was that my mother was always convinced that you mustn't let it get to you. You have to defend yourself! When my teachers made anti-Semitic remarks—mostly not about me, but about other Jewish girls, eastern Jewish students in particular—I was told to get up immediately, leave the classroom, come home, and report everything exactly. Then my mother wrote one of her many registered letters; and for me the matter was completely settled. I had a day off from school, and that was marvelous! But when it came from children, I was not permitted to tell about it at home. That didn't count. You defended yourself against what came from children. Thus these matters never were a problem for me. There were rules of conduct by which I retained my dignity, so to speak, and I was protected, absolutely protected, at home.

GAUS: You studied in Marburg, Heidelberg, and Freiberg with professors Heidegger, Bultmann, and Jaspers; with a major in philosophy and minors in theology and Greek. How did you come to choose these subjects?

ARENDT: You know, I have often thought about that. I can only say that I always knew I would study philosophy. Ever since I was fourteen years old.

GAUS: Why?

ARENDT: I read Kant. You can ask, Why did you read Kant?

For me the question was somehow: I can either study philosophy or I can drown myself, so to speak. But not because I didn't love life! No! As I said before—I had this need to understand . . . The need to understand was there very early. You see, all the books were in the library at home; one simply took them from the shelves.

GAUS: Besides Kant, do you remember special experiences in reading?

ARENDT: Yes. First of all, Jaspers's *Psychologie der Weltanschauungen* (*Psychology of Worldviews*), published, I believe, in 1920.* I was fourteen. Then I read Kierkegaard, and that fit together.

GAUS: Is this where theology came in?

ARENDT: Yes. They fit together in such a way that for me they both belonged together. I had some misgivings only as to how one deals with this if one is Jewish . . . how one proceeds. I had no idea, you know. I had difficult problems that were then resolved by themselves. Greek is another matter. I have always loved Greek poetry. And poetry has played a large role in my life. So I chose Greek in addition. It was the easiest thing to do, since I read it anyway!

GAUS: I am impressed!

---

* Karl Jaspers's *Psychologie der Weltanschauungen* was first published in Berlin in 1919.

ARENDT: No, you exaggerate.

GAUS: Your intellectual gifts were tested so early, Miss Arendt. Did it sometimes separate you as a schoolgirl and as a young student from the usual day-to-day relationships, painfully perhaps?

ARENDT: That would have been the case had I known about it. I thought everybody was like that.

GAUS: When did you realize you were wrong?

ARENDT: Rather late. I don't want to say how late. I am embarrassed. I was indescribably naive. That was partly due to my upbringing at home. Grades were never discussed. That was taken to be inferior. Any ambition was taken to be inferior. In any case, the situation wasn't at all clear to me. I experienced it sometimes as a sort of strangeness among people.

GAUS: A strangeness which you believed came from you?

ARENDT: Yes, exclusively. But that has nothing to do with talent. I never connected it with talent.

GAUS: Was the result sometimes disdain for others in your youth?

ARENDT: Yes, that happened. Very early. And I have often suffered because I felt such disdain, that is, knowing one really shouldn't, and one really must not, and so forth.

GAUS: When you left Germany in 1933, you went to Paris, where you worked in an organization that tried to provide for Jewish youngsters in Palestine. Can you tell me something about that?

ARENDT: This organization brought Jewish youngsters between thirteen and seventeen from Germany to Palestine and housed them there in kibbutzim. For this reason, I really know these settlements pretty well.

GAUS: And from a very early period.

ARENDT: From a very early period; at that time I had a lot of respect for them. The children received vocational training and retraining. Sometimes I also smuggled in Polish children. It was regular social work, educational work. There were large camps in the country where the children were prepared for Palestine, where they also had lessons, where they learned farming, where they above all had to gain weight. We had to clothe them from head to foot. We had to cook for them. Above all, we had to get papers for them, we had to deal with the parents—and before everything else we had to get money for them. That was also largely my job. I worked together with French women. That is more or less what we did. Do you want to hear how I decided to take on this work?

GAUS: Please.

ARENDT: You see, I came out of a purely academic background. In this respect the year 1933 made a very lasting impression on me. First a positive one and then a negative one. Perhaps I had better say first a negative one and then a positive one. People often think today that German Jews were shocked in 1933 because Hitler assumed power. As far as I and people of my generation are concerned, I can say that that is a curious misunderstanding. Naturally Hitler's rise was very bad. But it was political. It wasn't personal. We didn't need Hitler's assumption of power to know that the Nazis were our enemies! That had been completely evident for at least four years to everyone who wasn't feebleminded. We also knew that a large number of the German people were behind them. That could not shock us or surprise us in 1933.

GAUS: You mean that the shock in 1933 came from the fact that events went from the generally political to the personal?

ARENDT: Not even that. Or, that too. First of all, the generally political became a personal fate when one emigrated. Second . . . friends "coordinated" or got in line. The problem, the personal problem, was not what our enemies did but what our friends did. In the wave of *Gleichschaltung* (coordination),* which was relatively voluntary—in any case, not yet under the pressure of terror—it was as if an empty space formed

---

* *Gleichschaltung*, or political co-ordination, refers to the widespread giving in, at the outset of the Nazi era, to the changed political climate in order either to secure one's position or to get employment. In addition, it describes the Nazi policy of converting traditional organizations—youth groups and all sorts of clubs and associations— into specifically Nazi organizations.

around one. I lived in an intellectual milieu, but I also knew other people. And among intellectuals *Gleichschaltung* was the rule, so to speak. But not among the others. And I never forgot that. I left Germany dominated by the idea—of course somewhat exaggerated: Never again! I shall never again get involved in any kind of intellectual business. I want nothing to do with that lot. Also I didn't believe then that Jews and German Jewish intellectuals would have acted any differently had their own circumstances been different. That was not my opinion. I thought that it had to do with this profession, with being an intellectual. I am speaking in the past tense. Today I know more about it . . .

GAUS: I was just about to ask you if you still believe that.

ARENDT: No longer to the same degree. But I still think that it belongs to the essence of being an intellectual that one fabricates ideas about everything. No one ever blamed someone if he "coordinated" because he had to take care of his wife or child. The worst thing was that some people really believed in Nazism! For a short time, many for a very short time. But that means that they made up ideas about Hitler, in part terrifically interesting things! Completely fantastic and interesting and complicated things! Things far above the ordinary level! I found that grotesque. Today I would say that they were trapped by their own ideas. That is what happened. But then, at that time, I didn't see it so clearly.

GAUS: And that was the reason that it was particularly

important for you to get out of intellectual circles and start to do work of a practical nature?

ARENDT: Yes. The positive side is the following. I realized what I then expressed time and again in the sentence: If one is attacked as a Jew, one must defend oneself as a Jew. Not as a German, not as a world citizen, not as an upholder of the Rights of Man, or whatever. But: What can I specifically do as a Jew? Second, it was now my clear intention to work with an organization. For the first time. To work with the Zionists. They were the only ones who were ready. It would have been pointless to join those who had assimilated. Besides, I never really had anything to do with them. Even before this time I had concerned myself with the Jewish question. The book on Rahel Varnhagen was finished when I left Germany.* The problem of the Jews plays a role in it. I wrote it with the idea, "I want to understand." I wasn't discussing my personal problems as a Jew. But now, belonging to Judaism had become my own problem, and my own problem was political. Purely political! I wanted to go into practical work, exclusively and only Jewish work. With this in mind I then looked for work in France.

GAUS: Until 1940.

ARENDT: Yes.

---

* Except for the last two chapters, which were written sometime between 1933 and 1936 in France. *Rahel Varnhagen: The Life of a Jewish Woman*, rev. ed. (New York: Harcourt Brace Jovanovich, 1974), xiii.

GAUS: Then during the Second World War you went to the United States of America, where you are now a professor of political theory, not philosophy . . .

ARENDT: Thank you.

GAUS: . . . in Chicago. You live in New York. Your husband, whom you married in 1940, is also a professor, of philosophy, in America. The academic community, of which you are again a member—after the disillusionment of 1933—is international. Yet I should like to ask you whether you miss the Europe of the pre-Hitler period, which will never exist again. When you come to Europe, what, in your impression, remains and what is irretrievably lost?

ARENDT: The Europe of the pre-Hitler period? I do not long for that, I can tell you. What remains? The language remains.

GAUS: And that means a great deal to you?

ARENDT: A great deal. I have always consciously refused to lose my mother tongue. I have always maintained a certain distance from French, which I then spoke very well, as well as from English, which I write today.

GAUS: I wanted to ask you that. You write in English now?

ARENDT: I write in English, but I have never lost a feeling of distance from it. There is a tremendous difference between your mother tongue and another language. For myself I can put it extremely simply: In German I know a rather large part of German poetry by heart; the poems are always somehow in the back of my mind. I can never do that again. I do things in German that I would not permit myself to do in English. That is, sometimes I do them in English too, because I have become bold, but in general I have maintained a certain distance. The German language is the essential thing that has remained and that I have always consciously preserved.

GAUS: Even in the most bitter time?

ARENDT: Always. I thought to myself, What is one to do? It wasn't the German language that went crazy. And, second, there is no substitution for the mother tongue. People can forget their mother tongue. That's true—I have seen it. There are people who speak the new language better than I do. I still speak with a very heavy accent, and I often speak unidiomatically. They can all do these things correctly. But they do them in a language in which one cliché chases another because the productivity that one has in one's own language is cut off when one forgets that language.

GAUS: The cases in which the mother tongue was forgotten: Is it your impression that this was the result of repression?

ARENDT: Yes, very frequently. I have seen it in people as a result of shock. You know, what was decisive was not the year 1933, at least not for me. What was decisive was the day we learned about Auschwitz.

GAUS: When was that?

ARENDT: That was in 1943. And at first we didn't believe it—although my husband and I always said that we expected anything from that bunch. But we didn't believe this because militarily it was unnecessary and uncalled for. My husband is a former military historian, he understands something about these matters. He said don't be gullible, don't take these stories at face value. They can't go that far! And then a half year later we believed it after all, because we had the proof. That was the real shock. Before that we said: Well, one has enemies. That is entirely natural. Why shouldn't a people have enemies? But this was different. It was really as if an abyss had opened. Because we had the idea that amends could somehow be made for everything else, as amends can be made for just about everything at some point in politics. But not for this. *This ought not to have happened.* And I don't mean just the number of victims. I mean the method, the fabrication of corpses and so on—I don't need to go into that. This should not have happened. Something happened there to which we cannot reconcile ourselves. None of us ever can. About everything else that happened I have to say that it was sometimes rather difficult: we were very poor, we were hunted down, we had to flee, by hook or by crook we somehow had to get through, and whatever. That's how it was. But we were young. I even had a little fun with it—I can't deny it. But not this. This was something completely different. Personally I could accept everything else.

GAUS: I should like to hear from you, Miss Arendt, how

your opinions about postwar Germany, which you have often
visited, and in which your most important works have been
published, have changed since 1945.

ARENDT: I returned to Germany for the first time in 1949, in
the service of a Jewish organization for the recovery of Jewish
cultural treasures, mostly books. I came with very good will.
My thoughts after 1945 were as follows: Whatever happened
in 1933 is really unimportant in light of what happened after that. Certainly, the disloyalty of friends, to put it bluntly
for once . . .

GAUS: . . . which you experienced personally . . .

ARENDT: Of course. But if someone really became a Nazi
and wrote articles about it, he did not have to be loyal to me
personally. I did not speak to him again anyhow. He didn't
have to get in touch with me anymore, because as far as I
was concerned he had ceased to exist. That much is clear. But
they were not all murderers. There were people who fell into
their own trap, as I would say today. Nor did they desire what
came later. Thus it seemed to me that there should be a basis for communication precisely in the abyss of Auschwitz.
And that was true in many personal relations. I argued with
people; I am not particularly agreeable, nor am I very polite; I
say what I think. But somehow things were set straight again
with a lot of people. As I said, all these were only people who
were committed to Nazism for a few months, at the worst
for a few years; neither murderers nor informers. People, as I
said, who "made up ideas" about Hitler. But the general, and

the greatest experience when one returns to Germany—apart from the experience of recognition, which is always the crux of the action in Greek tragedy—is one of violent emotion. And then there was the experience of hearing German spoken in the streets. For me that was an indescribable joy.

GAUS: This was your reaction when you came in 1949?

ARENDT: More or less. And today, now that things are back on track, the distance I feel has become greater than it was before, when I experienced things in that highly emotional state.

GAUS: Because conditions here got back on track too quickly in your opinion?

ARENDT: Yes. And often on a track to which I do not assent. But I don't feel responsible for that. I see it from the outside now. And that means that I am far less involved than I was at that time. That could be because of the lapse of time. Listen, fifteen years are not nothing!

GAUS: You have become much more indifferent?

ARENDT: Distant ... "indifferent" is too strong. But there is distance.

GAUS: Miss Arendt, your book on the trial of Eichmann in Jerusalem was published this fall in the Federal Republic. Since its publication in America, your book has been very heatedly discussed. From the Jewish side, especially, objections have been raised which you say are partly based on misunderstandings and partly on an intentional political campaign. Above all, people were offended by the question you raised about the extent to which Jews are to blame for their passive acceptance of the German mass murders, or to what extent the collaboration of certain Jewish councils almost constitutes a kind of guilt of their own. In any case, for a portrait of Hannah Arendt, so to speak, a number of questions come out of this book. If I may begin with them: Is the criticism that your book is lacking in love for the Jewish people painful to you?

ARENDT: First of all, I must, in all friendliness, state that you yourself have become a victim of this campaign. Nowhere in my book did I reproach the Jewish people with nonresistance. Someone else did that in the Eichmann trial, namely, Mr. Haussner of the Israeli public prosecutor's office. I called such questions directed to the witnesses in Jerusalem both foolish and cruel.

GAUS: I have read the book. I know that. But some of the criticisms made of you are based on the tone in which many passages are written.

ARENDT: Well, that is another matter. What can I say? Besides, I don't want to say anything. If people think that one can only write about these things in a solemn tone of voice . . . Look, there are people who take it amiss—and I can understand that in a sense—that, for instance, I can still laugh. But I was really of the opinion that Eichmann was a buffoon. I'll tell you this: I read the transcript of his police investigation, thirty-six hundred pages, read it, and read it very carefully, and I do not know how many times I laughed—laughed out loud! People took this reaction in a bad way. I cannot do anything about that. But I know one thing: three minutes before certain death, I probably still would laugh. And that, they say, is the tone of voice. That the tone of voice is predominantly ironic is completely true. The tone of voice in this case is really the person. When people reproach me with accusing the Jewish people, that is a malignant lie and propaganda and nothing else. The tone of voice, however, is an objection against me personally. And I cannot do anything about that.

GAUS: You are prepared to bear that?

ARENDT: Yes, willingly. What is one to do? I cannot say to people: You misunderstand me, and in truth this or that is going on in my heart. That's ridiculous.

GAUS: In this connection I should like to go back to a personal statement of yours. You said: "I have never in my life 'loved' any people or collective group, neither the German people, the French, the Americans, nor the working class or anything of that sort. I indeed love only my friends, and the only kind of love I know of and believe in is the love of persons. Moreover, this 'love of the Jews' would appear to me, since I am myself Jewish, as something rather suspect."* May I ask something? As a politically active being, doesn't man

* Arendt to Scholem, July 24, 1963.

need commitment to a group, a commitment that can then to a certain extent be called love? Are you not afraid that your attitude could be politically sterile?

ARENDT: No. I would say it is the other attitude that is politically sterile. In the first place, belonging to a group is a natural condition. You belong to some sort of group when you are born, always. But to belong to a group in the way you mean, in a second sense, that is, to join or form an organized group, is something completely different. This kind of organization has to do with a relation to the world. People who become organized have in common what are ordinarily called interests. The directly personal relationship, where one can speak of love, exists of course foremost in real love, and it also exists in a certain sense in friendship. There a person is addressed directly, independent of his relation to the world. Thus, people of the most divergent organizations can still be personal friends. But if you confuse these things, if you bring love to the negotiating table, to put it bluntly, I find that fatal.

GAUS: You find it apolitical?

ARENDT: I find it apolitical. I find it worldless. And I really find it to be a great disaster. I admit that the Jewish people are a classic example of a worldless people maintaining themselves throughout thousands of years . . .

GAUS: "World" in the sense of your terminology as space for politics.

ARENDT: As space for politics.

GAUS: Thus the Jewish people were an apolitical people?

ARENDT: I shouldn't say that exactly, for the communities were, of course, to a certain extent, also political. The Jewish religion is a national religion. But the concept of the political was valid only with great reservations. This worldlessness which the Jewish people suffered in being dispersed, and which—as with all people who are pariahs—generated a special warmth among those who belonged, changed when the state of Israel was founded.

GAUS: Did something get lost, then, something the loss of which you regret?

ARENDT: Yes, one pays dearly for freedom. The specifically Jewish humanity signified by their worldlessness was something very beautiful. You are too young to have ever experienced that. But it was something very beautiful, this standing outside of all social connections, the complete open-mindedness and absence of prejudice that I experienced, especially with my mother, who also exercised it in relation to the whole Jewish community. Of course, a great deal was lost with the passing of all that. One pays for liberation. I once said in my Lessing speech . . .

GAUS: Hamburg in 1959 . . .*

---

* Arendt's address on accepting the Lessing Prize of the Free City of Hamburg is reprinted as "On Humanity in Dark Times: Thoughts About Lessing," in *Men in Dark Times* (New York: Harcourt, Brace & World, 1968).

ARENDT: Yes, there I said that "this humanity . . . has never yet survived the hour of liberation, of freedom, by so much as a minute." You see, that has also happened to us.

GAUS: You wouldn't like to undo it?

ARENDT: No. I know that one has to pay a price for freedom. But I cannot say that I like to pay it.

GAUS: Miss Arendt, do you feel that it is your duty to publish what you learn through political-philosophical speculation or sociological analysis? Or are there reasons to be silent about something you know?

ARENDT: Yes, that is a very difficult problem. It is at bottom the sole question that interested me in the whole controversy over the Eichmann book. But it is a question that never arose unless I broached it. It is the only serious question—everything else is pure propaganda soup. So, *fiat veritas, et pereat mundus* [let truth be told though the world may perish]?* But the Eichmann book did not de facto touch upon such things. The book really does not jeopardize anybody's legitimate interests. It was only thought to do so.

GAUS: You must leave the question of what is legitimate open to discussion.

---

* Arendt plays with the old Latin adage *Fiat iustitia, et periat mundus* (Let justice be done, though the world may perish). See also *Between Past and Future* (New York: Viking Press, 1968), 228.

ARENDT: Yes, that is true. You are right. The question of what is legitimate is still open to discussion. I probably mean by "legitimate" something different from what the Jewish organizations mean. But let us assume that real interests, which even I recognize, were at stake.

GAUS: Might one then be silent about the truth?

ARENDT: Might I have been? Yes! To be sure, I might have written it ... But look here, someone asked me, if I had anticipated one thing or another, wouldn't I have written the Eichmann book differently? I answered: No. I would have confronted the alternative: to write or not to write. Because one can also hold one's tongue.

GAUS: Yes.

ARENDT: One doesn't always have to speak. But now we come to the question of what, in the eighteenth century, were called "truths of fact." This is really a matter of truths of fact. It is not a matter of opinions. The historical sciences in the universities are the guardians of truths of fact.

GAUS: They have not always been the best ones.

ARENDT: No. They collapse. They are controlled by the state. I have been told that a historian remarked of some book about the origin of the First World War: "I won't let this spoil the memory of such an uplifting time!" That is a man who does not know who he is. But that is uninteresting. De facto he is the guardian of historical truth, the truth of facts. And we know how important these guardians are from Bolshevik history, for example, where history is rewritten every five years and the facts remain unknown: for instance, that there was a Mr. Trotsky. Is this what we want? Is that what governments are interested in?

GAUS: They might have that interest. But do they have that right?

ARENDT: Do they have that right? They do not appear to believe it themselves—otherwise they would not tolerate universities at all. Thus, even states are interested in the truth. I don't mean military secrets; that's something else. But these events go back approximately twenty years. Why shouldn't one speak the truth?

GAUS: Perhaps because twenty years are still too little?

ARENDT: Many people say that; others say that after twenty years one can no longer figure out the truth. In any case, there is an interest in whitewashing. That, however, is not a legitimate interest.

GAUS: In case of doubt, you would prefer the truth.

ARENDT: I would rather say that impartiality—which came into the world when Homer . . .

GAUS: For the conquered as well . . .

ARENDT: Right!

Wenn des Liedes Stimmen schweigen
Von dem überwundnen Mann,
So will ich für Hectorn zeugen . . .

[If the voices of song are silent
For him who has been vanquished,
I myself will testify for Hector . . .]*

Isn't that right? That's what Homer did. Then came
Herodotus, who spoke of "the great deeds of the Greeks *and*
the barbarians." All of science comes from this spirit, even
modern science, and the science of history too. If someone is
not capable of this impartiality because he pretends to love his
people so much that he pays flattering homage to them all the
time—well, then there's nothing to be done. I do not believe
that people like that are patriots.

GAUS: In one of your most important works, *The Human
Condition*, you come to the conclusion, Miss Arendt, that
the modern period has dethroned the sense of what concerns
everyone, that is, the sense of the prime importance of the
political. You designate as modern social phenomena the up-
rooting and loneliness of the masses and the triumph of a type
of human being who finds satisfaction in the process of mere
labor and consumption. I have two questions about this.
First, to what extent is this kind of philosophical knowledge

* From Schiller's *Das Siegesfest*.

dependent upon a personal experience which first gets the process of thinking going?

ARENDT: I do not believe that there is any thought process possible without personal experience. Every thought is an afterthought, that is, a reflection on some matter or event. Isn't that so? I live in the modern world, and obviously my experience is in and of the modern world. This, after all, is not controversial. But the matter of merely laboring and consuming is of crucial importance for the reason that a kind of worldlessness defines itself there too. Nobody cares any longer what the world looks like.

GAUS: "World" understood always as the space in which politics can originate.

ARENDT: I comprehend it now in a much larger sense, as the space in which things become public, as the space in which one lives and which must look presentable. In which art appears, of course. In which all kinds of things appear. You remember that Kennedy tried to expand the public space quite decisively by inviting poets and other ne'er-do-wells to the White House. So that it all could belong to this space. However, in labor and consumption man is utterly thrown back on himself.

GAUS: On the biological.

ARENDT: On the biological, and on himself. And there you have the connection with loneliness. A peculiar loneliness arises in the process of labor. I cannot go into that right now, because it would lead us too far afield. But this loneliness consists in being thrown back upon oneself; a state of affairs in which, so to speak, consumption takes the place of all the truly relating activities.

GAUS: A second question in this connection: In *The Human Condition* you come to the conclusion that "truly world-oriented experiences"—you mean insights and experiences of the highest political significance—"withdraw more and more from the experiential horizon of the average human life." You say that today "the ability to act is restricted to a few people." What does this mean in terms of practical politics, Miss Arendt? To what extent does a form of government based, at least theoretically, on the cooperative responsibility of all citizens become a fiction under these circumstances?

ARENDT: I want to qualify that a bit. Look, this inability to be realistically oriented applies not only to the masses, but also to every other stratum of society. I would say even to the statesman. The statesman is surrounded, encircled by an army of experts. So that now the question of action lies between the statesman and the experts. The statesman has to make the final decision. He can hardly do that realistically, since he can't know everything himself. He must take the advice of experts, indeed of experts who in principle always have to contradict each other. Isn't that so? Every reasonable statesman summons experts with opposing points of view. Because he has to see the matter from all sides. That's true, isn't it? He has to judge between them. And this judging is a highly mysterious process—in which, then, common sense* is made manifest. As far as the masses are concerned, I would say the following: Wherever men come together, in whatever numbers, public interests come into play.

GAUS: Always.

ARENDT: And the public realm is formed. In America where there are still spontaneous associations, which then disband again—the kind of associations already described by Tocqueville—you can see this very clearly. Some public interest concerns a specific group of people, those in a neighborhood or even in just one house or in a city or in some other sort of group. Then these people will convene, and they are very capable of acting publicly in these matters—for they have an overview of them. What you were aiming at with your question applies only to the greatest decisions on the highest level. And, believe me, the difference between the statesman and the man in the street is in principle not very great.

GAUS: Miss Arendt, you have been in close contact with Karl Jaspers, your former teacher, in an ongoing dialogue. What do you think is the greatest influence that Professor Jaspers has had on you?

* By "common sense" (*Gemeinsinn*), Arendt does not mean the unreflective prudence that every sane adult exercises continuously (*gesunder Menschenverstand*), but, rather, as Kant put it, "a sense *common to all* . . . a faculty of judgment which, in its reflection, takes account . . . of the mode of representation of all other men," Immanuel Kant, *Critique of Judgment*, §40, cited in Arendt's *Lectures on Kant's Political Philosophy*, ed. R. Beiner (Chicago: University of Chicago Press, 1982), 70–72.

ARENDT: Well, where Jaspers comes forward and speaks, all becomes luminous. He has an unreservedness, a trust, an unconditionality of speech that I have never known in anyone else. This impressed me even when I was very young. Besides, he has a conception of freedom linked to reason which was completely foreign to me when I came to Heidelberg. I knew nothing about it, although I had read Kant. I saw this reason in action, so to speak. And if I may say so—I grew up without a father—I was educated by it. I don't want to make him responsible for me, for God's sake, but if anyone succeeded in instilling some sense in me, it was he. And this dialogue is, of course, quite different today. That was really my most powerful postwar experience. That there can be such conversations! That one can speak in such a way!

GAUS: Permit me a last question. In a tribute to Jaspers you said: "Humanity is never acquired in solitude, and never by giving one's work to the public. It can be achieved only by one who has thrown his life and his person into the 'venture into the public realm.' "* This "venture into the public realm"— which is a quotation from Jaspers—what does it mean for Hannah Arendt?

ARENDT: The venture into the public realm seems clear to me. One exposes oneself to the light of the public, as a person. Although I am of the opinion that one must not appear and act in public self-consciously, still I know that in every action the person is expressed as in no other human activity. Speaking

* "Karl Jaspers: A Laudatio," in *Men in Dark Times*, 73–74.

is also a form of action. That is one venture. The other is: We start something. We weave our strand into a network of relations. What comes of it we never know. We've all been taught to say: Lord forgive them, for they know not what they do. That is true of all action. Quite simply and concretely true, because one *cannot* know. That is what is meant by a venture. And now I would say that this venture is only possible when there is trust in people. A trust—which is difficult to formulate but fundamental—in what is human in all people. Otherwise such a venture could not be made.

"EICHMANN WAS OUTRAGEOUSLY STUPID"

INTERVIEW BY JOACHIM FEST
DAS THEMA, SWR TV, GERMANY
NOVEMBER 9, 1964

TRANSLATED BY ANDREW BROWN

FEST: Frau Arendt, do you think there is any connection between the Eichmann trial and the so-called concentration camp trials* in Germany? And in particular, are the reactions in Germany and Israel in any way comparable? People have occasionally suggested that Germans and Jews have in common what is called—in a somewhat inadequate expression—an "unmastered past."

ARENDT: Well, those are actually two questions. Perhaps I might answer the first one first: in my view, the Eichmann trial has really acted as a catalyst for the trials in Germany. Some of these took place earlier, and some arrests were made earlier. But when you look at this from the statistical point of view and bear in mind the date of Eichmann's abduction, not the date of the Eichmann trial, of course, you'll be overwhelmed, purely in terms of percentages. And I don't want to say here why I think it was like this—it's just a fact.

Now you are quite right to say that the question of the unmastered past is something the Jews and Germans have

---

* Fest is referring here to a series of trials that ran from December 20, 1963, to August 19, 1965, in which a number of mid- and lower-level officials in the Auschwitz-Birkenau camp complex were tried for their crimes. The trials were notable for being largely open to the public, and they made many German citizens aware for the first time of the details and mechanisms of the Holocaust.

in common. I'd like to qualify that a bit. To begin with, of course, the actual kind of unmastered past that they have in common is very different in the case of victims and per petrators; for even the *Judenräte** were, of course, victims. This doesn't mean they are a hundred percent exonerated, but they obviously stand on the other side—that much is clear.

Now the unmastered past is also something that—I know this from America—Jews and Germans actually share with almost all countries or all peoples on earth, at least in Europe and America. The very horror that the whole business arouses affects everyone, not just Jews and Germans. What Jews and Germans have in common is the fact that they are the ones immediately involved.

And now you ask, "Is this reaction the same in Germany and Israel?" Look, a quarter of the population of Israel, twenty-five percent, consists of people who were immediately involved. That's a huge percentage in a population. That they, as victims, obviously react differently from the average German of any generation, who has only one wish—never to hear anything more about it—is clear. But *they* don't want to hear about it either; but for completely different reasons.

Now there's one thing that I've noticed, and that's the attitude of the younger generation in Israel and of those born in that country. And there's a lack of interest that's similar in some ways to the lack of interest in Germany. In Israel, they also feel, "It's our parents' problem" ... Only now, of course, it's different: "If our parents want this or that to happen ...

* Jewish councils, the administrative bodies of Jewish communities.

well, of course! They're welcome! But they should please leave
us out of it . . . We're not very interested in that." This was a
really general feeling. So it's a generational problem, as it is
in Germany.

FEST: These trials—like the Nuremberg Trials, to some extent, and the associated trials held mainly in Nuremberg—
have brought to light a new type of criminal.

ARENDT: It is indeed a new type of criminal, I agree with
you on that, though I'd like to qualify it. When we think
of a criminal, we imagine someone with criminal motives.
And when we look at Eichmann, he doesn't actually have any
criminal motives. Not what is usually understood by "criminal motives." He wanted to go along with the rest. He wanted
to say "we," and going-along-with-the-rest and wanting-to-
say-we like this were quite enough to make the greatest of all
crimes possible. The Hitlers, after all, really aren't the ones
who are typical in this kind of situation—they'd be powerless
without the support of others.

So what's actually going on here? I'd like to concentrate
just on Eichmann, since I know him well. And the first thing
I'd like to say, you see, is that going along with the rest—
the kind of going along that involves lots of people acting
together—produces power. So long as you're alone, you're
always powerless, however strong you may be. This feeling
of power that arises from acting together is absolutely not
wrong in itself, it's a general human feeling. But it's not good,
either. It's simply neutral. It's something that's simply a phenomenon, a general human phenomenon that needs to be

described as such. In acting in this way, there's an extreme feeling of pleasure. I won't start quoting reams of material here—you could go on quoting examples from the American Revolution for hours at a time. And I'd say that the really perverse form of acting is functioning, and in this functioning the feeling of pleasure is always there. Yet everything in action is also there in acting together with others, namely, in discussing things together, reaching certain decisions, accepting responsibility, thinking about what we are doing—all of which is eliminated in functioning. What you have there is mere freewheeling. And the pleasure in this mere functioning—this pleasure was quite evident in Eichmann. Did he take particular pleasure in power? I don't think so. He was a typical functionary. And a functionary, when he really is nothing more than a functionary, is really a very dangerous gentleman. Ideology, in my view, didn't play a very big role here. This seems to me the decisive factor.

FEST: When I mentioned a new type of criminal, I meant the following kind of situation: there was a tendency after the war, both in Germany and in the allied countries, to demonize the leaders in the Third Reich. The Germans always saw these figures, from Hitler right down to Eichmann, as beasts from the depths and they possibly understood this as a way of creating a certain alibi for themselves. If you succumb to the power of a beast from the depths, you're naturally much less guilty than if you succumb to a completely average man of the caliber of an Eichmann.

ARENDT: And it is much more interesting.

FEST: Really? Okay. The situation with the Allies was quite similar. In that case, they found a partial excuse for their lack of resolve, their appeasement policy up until 1939. And on the other hand, victory over this beast from the depths appears as much more glorious, when you're dealing with the Devil incarnate.

ARENDT: The demonization of Hitler, in my view, was much more common among the Germans, including the German émigrés, than among the Allies themselves. In fact, the Allies were appalled, immeasurably appalled, to an unprecedented degree, when the truth came to light. This is underrated in Germany, to a catastrophic degree. I mean they were profoundly shaken, to the core of their being, when they learnt about it, when an ordinary soldier saw Bergen-Belsen and so on ... I've experienced this in countless conversations. I've lived abroad—so I can tell you ...

Well, demonization itself can help, as you've rightly said, to provide an alibi. You succumb to the Devil incarnate, and as a result you're not guilty yourself. But above all ... Look here, our whole mythology or our whole tradition sees the Devil as a fallen angel. And the fallen angel is of course much more interesting than the angel who always remained an angel, since the latter doesn't even provide you with a good story. In other words, evil, especially in the twenties and thirties, played the role of ensuring that it alone had authentic depth, don't you think? And then you get the same situation in philosophy—the negative as the only thing that gives any impetus to history, and so on. You can pursue this idea a very long way. And as a result, if you demonize someone, not only do you make yourself look interesting, you also secretly ascribe to yourself a depth that other people don't have. The others are too superficial to have killed anyone in the gas chambers. Now I've put it like that deliberately, of course, but that's what it comes down to. Anyway, if there was ever anyone who deprived himself of any demonic aura, it was Herr Eichmann.

FEST: Eichmann was actually such a small figure that one observer asked whether they hadn't caught and put on trial the wrong man. And actually he wasn't a cruel man—this emerges quite unambiguously from all the documents. Quite the opposite: he always found it difficult to do what he was instructed to do, and from the fact that he always found it especially difficult, he derived a feeling of worth.

ARENDT: Yes. That's true, and unfortunately it's very common. You think that you can judge what's good or evil from whether you enjoy doing it or not. You think that evil is what always appears in the form of a temptation, while good is what you never spontaneously want to do. I think this is all total rubbish, if you don't mind me saying so. Brecht is always showing the temptation towards good as something that you have to withstand. If you go back into political theory, you can read the same thing in Machiavelli, and even in a certain sense in Kant. So Eichmann and many other people were very often tempted to do what we call good. They withstood it precisely because it was a temptation.

FEST: Yes, you've already indicated that the way we imagine evil, or the way evil is imagined and has been formulated in our culture, in religious, philosophical and literary terms, has no place for the type of man like Eichmann. One of the main ideas in your book—it already emerges from your subtitle—is the "banality of evil." This has led to many misunderstandings.

ARENDT: Yes, look here, these misunderstandings actually run through the whole polemic, they belong to the small part of it that is genuine. In other words, it's my view that these misunderstandings would have arisen in any case. Somehow, it shocked people enormously, and I can understand that perfectly well; I myself was very shocked by it, too. For me too, it was something for which I was quite unprepared.

Now, one misunderstanding is this: people thought that what is banal is also commonplace. But I thought ... That wasn't what I meant. I didn't in the least mean that there's an Eichmann in all of us, each of us has an Eichmann in him and the Devil knows what else. Far from it! I can perfectly well imagine talking to somebody, and they say to me something that I've never heard before, so it's not in the least commonplace. And I say, "That's really banal." Or I say, "That's not much good." That's the sense in which I meant it.

Now, banality was a phenomenon that really couldn't be overlooked. The phenomenon expressed itself in those frankly incredible clichés and turns of phrase that we heard over and over again. Let me tell you what I mean by banality, since in Jerusalem I remembered a story that Ernst Jünger once told and that I'd forgotten.

During the war, Ernst Jünger came across some peasants

in Pomerania or Mecklenburg—no, I think it was Pomerania (the story is told in *Strahlungen**), and a peasant had taken in Russian prisoners of war straight from the camps, and naturally they were completely starving—you know how Russian prisoners of war were treated here. And he says to Jünger, "Well, they're subhuman—and [. . .] like cattle! It's easy to see: they eat the pigs' food." Jünger comments on this story, "It's sometimes as if the German people were being ridden by the Devil." And he didn't mean anything "demonic" by that. You see, there's something outrageously stupid about this story. I mean the story is stupid, so to speak. The man doesn't see that this is just what starving people do, right? And anyone would behave like that. But there's something really outrageous about this stupidity. [. . .] Eichmann was perfectly intelligent, but in this respect he was stupid. It was this stupidity that was so outrageous. And that was what I actually meant by banality. There's nothing deep about it—nothing demonic! There's simply the reluctance ever to imagine what the other person is experiencing, right?

FEST: Would you say that Eichmann, and Höß[†] too, are specifically German figures? You mentioned Kant just now, and Eichmann himself occasionally referred to Kant during his trial. He's supposed to have said that he had followed Kant's

---

* *Strahlungen* (Radiation) was the title of Ernst Jünger's collected diaries from the Second World War, first published in 1949.
[†] Rudolf Höß, commandant of Auschwitz from mid-May 1940 through November 1943.

moral precepts all his life long, and made Kant's concept of duty his guiding principle.

ARENDT: Yes. Quite an impertinent remark, of course, isn't it? On Herr Eichmann's part. After all, Kant's whole ethics amounts to the idea that every person, in every action, must reflect on whether the maxim of his action can become a general law. In other words . . . It really is the complete opposite, so to speak, of obedience! Each person is a lawgiver. In Kant, nobody has the right to obey. The only thing that Eichmann did take from Kant is that fatal business of inclination.* And this is, unfortunately, very widespread in Germany. This curious concept of duty in Germany . . . I'll say this to you: Look here, Hitler or sadists such as Boger in the Auschwitz trial,† Hitler was probably just a murderer with murderous instincts. In my opinion, these people aren't typical Germans.

In my view, the Germans as a people aren't especially brutal. In fact, I do not believe in such national characteristics . . . Still, the story I told just now, Jünger's story, is specifically German. I mean this inability, as Kant says, if I can now really quote his own words, "to think in the place of every other person"—yes, the inability . . . This kind of stupidity, it's like talking to a brick wall. You never get any reaction, because these people never pay any attention to you. That

---

* In Kant's moral philosophy, the concepts of inclination and duty are always opposed.

† Wilhelm Boger, a police commissioner and concentration camp overseer, was infamous for his brutality while serving in the political department at Auschwitz. He was tried in the Frankfurt Auschwitz trials of 1965 and sentenced to life imprisonment.

is German. The second thing that strikes me as specifically German is this frankly crazy way that obedience is idealized. We obey in this sense when we're children, when it is necessary. Obedience is a very important matter then. But this should come to an end at the age of fourteen, or at the latest fifteen.

FEST: Don't you think that behind the references to "oaths," "orders," "obedience" there's more than a mere excuse? Eichmann was forever referring to these words. He explained that he'd been brought up to be obedient from an early age; he asked, "What advantage would I have derived from disobedience? In what respect would it have been of any use to me?" And then he stated that when, in May 1945, no more orders were reaching him, he was suddenly overwhelmed by the feeling that the world was coming to an end.

ARENDT: A life without a leader!*

FEST: The problem of obedience runs like a leitmotif through his whole life—you can read it in the trial records, for instance, it's forever cropping up. It's really like the leitmotif of a completely sham existence.

ARENDT: Yes, this sham existence can of course be seen everywhere. But, you know, he wasn't the only person to refer to all that, was he? To "orders," "oaths," "God," "the duty to obey,"

* The word Arendt uses for "leader" is *Führer*.

and "obedience is a virtue." Also, Eichmann talked about "slavish obedience." In Jerusalem he got into a terrible muddle and suddenly said it was just a question of obeying slavishly, there was nothing good about it at all, and so on. Right? So it's forever whirling round and round in people's minds. No, the reference to "oaths," and the idea that responsibility has been taken from you, and so on—you don't find this just with Eichmann, I've also found it in the records of the Nuremberg Trials—there's something outrageously stupid about this too. You see, Eichmann produced these attacks of rage—as did the others—and said, "But they promised us that we wouldn't be held responsible. And now we're left holding the bag, aren't we? And what about the big fish? They've evaded responsibility, of course—as usual." Now you know how they evaded responsibility: either they took their own lives, or they were hanged. Not to remember this when you say something of the kind is grotesque. The whole thing is simply comical! Yes, in fact, they . . . they're no longer among the living! When you're unable to remember that all this is only relevant so long as people are still alive—well, in that case there's no helping you.

FEST: But to what extent is there a deeper problem lurking here? To what extent can people living in totalitarian circumstances still be held responsible? This doesn't apply just to the Eichmann type, it applies in the same way to the *Judenräte* on the other side.

ARENDT: Just a moment before I answer that question. Look, it's a really amazing phenomenon: none of these people expressed any remorse. Yes, Frank* did, obviously; perhaps Heydrich[†] on his deathbed—so they say; Ley[‡] . . .

FEST: Yes, in Frank's case I'd say it was a purely emotional remorse. He then retracted it straightaway in his concluding speech to the court.

ARENDT: Yes!

FEST: It was a very ambiguous feeling.

ARENDT: So I can say, "No one expressed remorse."

FEST: Basically, at any rate, it can't be definitely proved in a single case.

ARENDT: And, as is well known, Eichmann said, "Remorse is for little children." No one expressed remorse. On the other hand, we should imagine that when nobody expresses re-

---

* Hans Frank, the chief jurist of Nazi Germany and governor general of the "General Government" territory, which encompassed much of central and southern Poland as well as western Ukraine, during the war. He was tried at Nuremberg for war crimes and crimes against humanity, found guilty, and executed in 1946.

[†] Reinhard Heydrich, a high-ranking Nazi official and one of the principal architects of the Final Solution. He was attacked in Prague on May 27, 1942, by a team of Czech and Slovak soldiers, sent by the Czechoslovak government in exile, and died from his injuries a week later.

[‡] Robert Ley, Nazi politician and head of the German Labor Front from 1933 to 1945. He committed suicide in 1945, while awaiting trial for war crimes in Nuremberg.

morse, there ought to be at least one person who stands up for his actions and says, "Yes, actually, we did do it, for this and that reason, I still think the same way today. We lost. Whether we won or lost doesn't affect the cause itself." In actual fact, the case collapsed like a wet dishrag. And nobody did stand up. Nobody put forward any defense. And this seems quite crucial for the phenomenon you touched on just now—obedience. Don't you think? In other words: they just wanted to go along. They're ready to go along with everything. When someone says to them, "You're only one of us if you commit murder with us"—fine. When they're told, "You're only one of us if you *never* commit murder"—that's fine too. Right? That's the way I see it.

FEST: That is so true—indeed, Eichmann stated, when he was imprisoned by the Americans, that he'd been glad to submit to somebody else's leadership again. And the peculiar way he was ready to tell the court or rather the interrogation, the preliminary interrogation, everything he knew, is probably to be interpreted in the same way as his readiness to give absolute obedience to any current authority, right to the limit of what was possible—his readiness to submit to any authority.

ARENDT: Incredible. He felt wonderfully happy in Jerusalem. There's no question about it, is there? The superior was Landau,* everyone could see that, and then came various

---

* Moshe Landau, the presiding judge in the Eichmann trial, himself a refugee from Nazi Germany.

other ranks down to Herr Captain Less,* whom he used—as
Herr Mulisch rightly said†—as a father confessor. He said,
"Captain, I'll willingly say everything." Of course, he wanted
to cut a fine figure too. At any rate, tell his life story. Anyway,
the question of responsibility—shall we get back to that?

FEST: Yes, please.

ARENDT: You see, when we put people on trial, we ascribe
responsibility to them. And we have a right to do so, from the
legal standpoint ... We have the right, since the alternative
was not martyrdom. There was an alternative, on both sides:
you didn't have to go along, you could make up your own
mind. "Thanks anyway, but ... I'm not going along. I'm not
risking my life, I'm trying to get away, I'm trying to see if I can
slip off." Isn't that right? "But I'm not going along with anyone. And if I should be forced to go along, then I'll take my
own life." This possibility existed. It meant not saying "we,"
but "I"—judging for oneself. And judging for oneself is what
people did do, everywhere, at every level of the populace:
religious people and nonreligious people, old and young, educated and uneducated, nobles and bourgeois and very many
workers, an amazing number of workers, especially in Berlin,
where I was able to watch it happening.

Those who did go along always justified themselves the

---

* Captain Avner W. Less, a young Israeli police official who interrogated
Eichmann for 275 hours in the pretrial interrogations in 1961.
† Arendt is referring to Dutch journalist Harry Mulisch's book on the
Eichmann trial, *Strafsache 40/61* (*Criminal Case 40/61*), which she greatly
admired.

same way, as we can see. They always said, "We only stayed on so that things wouldn't get any worse." Right? But, well—this justification should be rejected once and for all—it *couldn't* have got any worse.

FEST: And the American prosecutor Jackson* at the Nuremberg Trials spoke his mind on this in a very apt and characteristic way. Referring to Schacht and Papen,† he said, "If we ask these people why they went along with it for such a long time, then they say it was because they wanted to prevent anything worse. And if we ask them why everything turned out so badly, they say they had no power." At this point, everything really falls apart and their apologia becomes a mere excuse.

ARENDT: Yes. They were all functionaries, too.

FEST: Absolutely.

ARENDT: With scruples—they were functionaries with scruples. But their scruples didn't go far enough to show them clearly that there is a boundary at which human beings cease being just functionaries. And if they'd gone away and said, "For God's sake, let someone else do the dirty work!"—then

* Robert H. Jackson, the chief U.S. prosecutor at the Nuremberg Trials.
† Hjalmar Schacht, an economist, banker, and politician who served in Hitler's government as president of the Reichsbank and minister of economics; and Franz von Papen, a politician who served as vice-chancellor of Germany under Hitler in 1933 and 1934.

they'd suddenly have become human beings again, instead of functionaries, wouldn't they?

FEST: Yes. But I'd still like to ask once again what possibilities there were to remain guiltless in a totalitarian regime or in totalitarian circumstances. Many people are not heroes, and you can't expect them to be heroes. [...] But they're not criminals either, they're sometimes just accessories.

ARENDT: Yes, you know, it's a terrible thing being an accessory. The crucial aspect here, that people were guilty if they looked on, in other words if they didn't go along with it themselves or did immediately go along with it and then allowed themselves to be butchered, which was the impulse that drove a great many people ... As far as being an accessory is concerned, it was, I think, Jaspers who said the crucial thing. He said, "We are guilty of being alive."* Right? "For we could survive only by keeping our mouths shut." But you see, between this knowledge and the deed there's an abyss. Between the man who sees it and goes away and the man who does it. [...] So when the person who hasn't done anything, who has only seen and gone away, says, "We're all guilty," he thereby is covering up for the man who actually carried it through— this is what happened in Germany. And so we must not generalize this guilt, since that is only covering up for the guilty. Anyway, I'd like to say a bit more about this, if I may.

---

* Karl Jaspers, *Questions of German Guilt*, 2nd ed. (New York: Fordham University Press, 2000), 66.

FEST: Please do.

ARENDT: We need to realize that in totalitarian circumstances the phenomenon of powerlessness exists, and we need to realize that even in circumstances of absolute powerlessness there are still ways of behaving. In other words, it doesn't imply that you absolutely have to become a criminal. The phenomenon of powerlessness tips the scales, and this was of course the situation of all these people. They became absolutely powerless. There was no possibility of resisting, since they were all isolated, since they didn't belong together anywhere, since not even a dozen people could get together, as it were, and trust one another.

FEST: Would you say, Frau Arendt, that as regards this situation we can get by with the old, simple proposition that it's better to suffer injustice than to commit it?

ARENDT: Look, this proposition comes from Socrates. In our context, in other words, it was formulated before the religious commandments for Christian and western mankind, taken from the Jews, became authoritative. What Socrates always added, or rather Plato did, is that we can't prove this proposition. For some people, it's absolutely evident, and you can't prove to the other people that this is how they should behave. So what is the reason for the belief of those who view it as evident?

But there's another proposition of Socrates's, which in my view does provide us with the reason. It's this: "It is better to be in disunity with the whole world than with oneself, since I am a unity." For if I am not at unity with myself, a conflict arises that is unbearable. In other words, it's the idea of contradiction in the moral realm, and it's still authoritative for the categorical imperative in Kant. This idea presupposes that, in actual fact, I live with myself, and am so to speak two-in-one, so that I then say, "I will not do this or that." For I do not want to live with somebody who has done this. And then the only way out for me, if I had done this or that, would be suicide, or later, when thought of in Christian categories, changing my ways and showing remorse.

Now living with yourself means, of course, talking to yourself. And this talking-to-yourself is basically thinking—a kind of thinking that isn't technical, but a kind of which anybody is capable. So the presupposition behind the idea is: I can converse with myself. And so, there may be situations in which I become at disunity with the world to such an extent that I can only fall back on conversing with myself—and perhaps with a friend, too, with the other self, as Aristotle so beautifully put it: *autos allos*. This, in my view, is what powerlessness is actually like. And the people who walked away without doing anything were the ones who admitted to themselves that they were powerless and clung to this proposition, the proposition that someone who is powerless can still think.

FEST: Let's get back to Eichmann and the role that bureaucracy played in mass murder. What does it mean for an individual to be embedded in a bureaucratic apparatus? And how far does the awareness of injustice evaporate when you are part of an authority? Is it maybe that the merely partial responsibility given to a person hides the possibilities for any moral insight? Eichmann said, "I sat at my desk and did my work." And the former Gauleiter of Danzig stated that his official soul had always identified with what he did, but his private soul had always opposed it.*

ARENDT: Yes, this is the so-called internal emigration among the murderers—which means the extinction of the whole concept of inner emigration or inner resistance. I mean there's no such thing. There's only external resistance, inside there's at best a *Reservatio mentalis*, right? Those are the lies of a sham existence, transparent and rather nauseating. The bureaucracy, in other words, administered mass murder, which naturally created a sense of anonymity, as in any bureaucracy. The individual person is extinguished. As soon as the person concerned appears in front of the judge, he becomes a human being again. And this is actually what is so splendid about the legal system, isn't it? A real transformation takes place. For if the person then says, "But I was just a bureaucrat," the judge can say, "Hey, listen, that's not why you're here. You're standing here because you're a human being and because you did certain things." And there's something splendid about this transformation.

Apart from the fact that bureaucracy is essentially anonymous, any relentless activity allows responsibility to evaporate. There's an English idiom, "Stop and think." Nobody can

* Fest is referring here to Albert Forster, the Gauleiter (party leader of a regional branch of the NSDAP) of Danzig–West Prussia from 1935–1945. Forster was directly responsible for the mass murder, resettlement, and forced assimilation of tens of thousands of Jews and nonethnic Germans over the course of his administration.

think unless they stop. If you force someone into remorseless activity, or they allow themselves to be forced into it, it'll always be the same story, right? You'll always find that an awareness of responsibility can't develop. It can only develop in the moment when a person reflects—not on himself, but on what he's doing.

FEST: Let's turn for a moment to some of the legal consequences that arise from this whole complex, especially the question that's linked with what we've just been talking about: Does the Eichmann type still belong to the traditional concept of the murderer? Isn't he much more of a function in a murderous apparatus than a murderer? And does the partial responsibility he held justify the sense of total guilt?

ARENDT: We've already mentioned the murderer without a motive, I mean without the criminal motives we're familiar with: passion, self-interest ... Or the perpetrator who commits a crime out of conviction—an intermediate figure. All well and good! So in this sense the concepts we've inherited give us no handle. I'd say that this way of killing, from one's desk or in masses ... That is, of course, an incomparably more fearsome type of person than any ordinary murderer, since he no longer has any relationship with his victim at all. He really does kill people as if they were flies.

Partial responsibility was, of course, never a ground for partial guilt. Eichmann wasn't given the job of actually killing, since he wasn't suited for it. But he was part of the killing process! It's not important who actually does this or that. What I mean is ... when I say "But he's not a typical murderer," I don't mean that he's any better. What I mean is that he is infinitely worse, even though he has no actual "criminal instincts" as we call them. He was dragged into it all. But I can imagine murderers whom I might find, if I may say so, much more likeable than Herr Eichmann.

FEST: The court in Jerusalem also gave a conclusive answer to this question when it stated that in this case, it wasn't just a mass crime with regard to the victims that was at stake, but also one with regard to the perpetrators. Perhaps at this point I can quote: "Being near to or far away from . . . the man who actually kills the victim [can] have no influence on the extent of the responsibility . . . Rather, the degree of responsibility increases as we draw further away from the man who uses the fatal instrument with his own hands."*

ARENDT: Yes, quite true. I've quoted the same words myself. They come from the closing judgment. I entirely agree.

FEST: But the question is whether the legal norms in place can still grasp the nature of responsibility in this case. Would you say so?

ARENDT: Legal textbooks don't prepare us for administrative mass murder, and nothing prepares us for this type of perpetrator. So can we still exercise justice? Not in accordance with the legal textbooks, as it were, but de facto? In fact,

---

* See *Eichmann in Jerusalem* (New York: Viking Penguin, 1963), 247.

the judges—though they struggle with might and main to deny it—always passed judgment without any hindrance. [...]

Justice leads to two things. First, it should restore the order that has been disturbed. This is a process of healing that can only succeed if the ones who have disturbed order, the people we're talking about, are condemned. And second, in my view, is what affects us Jews . . . There's a quotation from Grotius that one of the judges used, but which they didn't pay much attention to, alas: he said that it is part of the honor and dignity of the person harmed or wounded that the perpetrator be punished. This has nothing to do with the suffering endured, it has nothing to do with putting something right. It's really a question of honor and dignity. Look, for us Jews it's a crucial question, when we're in Germany. If the German people think they can carry on living quite undisturbed with the murderers in their midst, this goes against the honor and dignity of the Jewish person.

FEST: Let's return to your book, Frau Arendt. In it, you referred to the way that the Eichmann trial laid bare the total nature of the moral collapse at the heart of Europe, among the persecutors and the persecuted alike, and in every country. Does the reaction to your book—a reaction that consisted on the one hand of denying this collapse, and on the other of making a confession of total guilt—indicate precisely what you were trying to prove?

ARENDT: Well, yes, this reaction to my book was for me . . . it was, of course, a test case—but after the event, not in the sense that I had expected it. Let me give you an example, one that I experienced several times ... This book was read in manuscript by a very great number of people (which is unusual for me), and of those people who read the book in manuscript, at least fifty percent, probably many more, were Jews. Not a single one of them voiced the reaction that came subsequently—they didn't even hint at it! In fact, these include, of course, people who are friends of mine and whom I know well. And one of them, for example, with this book ... not just one, but several Jews read the book in manuscript and were really enthusiastic, right? Then the campaign started up, and they completely forgot that they'd already read the book in manuscript. If you want to understand this phenomenon better—you know, this is yet another phenomenon—then you really must read *The Golden Fruits* by Nathalie Sarraute; she depicted it as a comedy. And it is indeed a comedy, it's the comedy of intellectual society, isn't it? The way these opinions swing this way and that, influenced of course by ... And many more people are subject to these influences than is generally realized. Aren't they? And this has absolutely nothing to do with intelligence. A person can be very intelligent and yet behave like that.

FEST: You mentioned the campaign. There are many reasons behind the resistance to the connections you drew in your book, of course, and some of them—it has to be said—deserve to be treated with respect. This raises the question: Should we tell the truth, even when we come into conflict with certain legitimate interests on the one hand, and people's feelings on the other?

ARENDT: Look, here you're touching on the only question in the whole controversy that is actually of interest to me.

I don't think that I damaged anyone's legitimate—let me emphasize *legitimate!*—interests. But let's assume that this is a controversial issue and that I did actually damage them. Should I have done so? Well, I think that such is the historians' task, as well as the task of people who live at that time and are independent—there are such people, and they need to be guardians of factual truths. What happens when these guardians are driven out by society, or driven into a corner or put up against a wall by the state—we've seen this happen in the writing of history, for example in Russia, where a new history of Russia comes out every five years. Does the state or society, with their legitimate interests that may come into conflict with the truth, still have an interest—in principle— with these guardians of factual truth? In this case I'd say yes. What then happens is of course that a whole series of apologias are brought out and put onto the market just to cover up the two or three truths that are actually quite marginal to this book. It won't succeed, as something of this kind never does.

But there's another thing: there are also legitimate feelings. And there's no question about it: I have wounded some people. And you know, it's somehow more unpleasant for me when I hurt people than when I get in the way of organizations and their interests, right? I take this seriously, I might say, but the other thing is more a matter of principle. Well, I have hurt these legitimate interests—essentially through my style, and I can't say much about that. You see, it's my view that the legitimate feeling here is sorrow. The *only* one! Not self-congratulation! And very few people understand this. There's nothing I can do about it. In fact, in my opinion people shouldn't adopt an emotional tone to talk about these things, since that's a way of playing them down. But all of that ... I also think that you must be able to laugh, since that's a form of sovereignty. And I feel that all these criticisms of my irony are very unpleasant, indeed, from the point of view of taste. But these are all personal matters. I'm obviously quite unpleasant in the eyes of a great many people. I can't do anything about that. What am I supposed to do? They just don't like me. The style in which people express themselves— well, that's something they themselves aren't aware of.

FEST: One last question, Frau Arendt. There were a great number of people who advised against publishing *Eichmann in Jerusalem* in Germany. They used phrases like "a negative impact on public awareness." How exactly could such a negative impact come about?

ARENDT: Well, the Jewish organizations quite obviously have an odd anxiety: they think that people might misuse my arguments. "That's it," they think, the anti-Semites are going to say "the Jews themselves were to blame." They say that anyway. But if you read my book, there's nothing that anti-Semites can use in it. And many people think the German people aren't mature yet. Well, if the German people aren't mature yet, then we'll probably have to wait until the Last Judgment.

THOUGHTS ON POLITICS AND REVOLUTION:
A COMMENTARY

INTERVIEW BY ADELBERT REIF
CRISES OF THE REPUBLIC
SUMMER 1970

TRANSLATED BY DENVER LINDLEY

REIF: In your study *On Violence** at several points you take up the question of the revolutionary student movement in the Western countries. In the end, though, one thing remains unclear: Do you consider the student protest movement in general a historically positive process?

ARENDT: I don't know what you mean by "positive." I assume you mean, am I for it or against it. Well, I welcome some of the goals of the movement, especially in America, where I am better acquainted with them than elsewhere; towards others I take a neutral attitude, and some I consider dangerous nonsense—as, for example, politicizing and "refunctioning" (what the Germans call *umfunktionieren*) the universities, that is, perverting their function, and other things of that sort. But not the right of participation. Within certain limits I thoroughly approve of that. But I don't want to go into that question for the moment.

If I disregard all the national differences, which of course are very great, and only take into account that this is a global movement—something that has never existed before in this

* *On Violence* was first published by Harcourt Brace Jovanovich in 1970. A few years later, it was included in the collection *Crises of the Republic* (New York: Harcourt Brace Jovanovich, 1972), where this interview first appeared in English.

form—and if I consider what (apart from goals, opinions, doctrines) really distinguishes this generation in all countries from earlier generations, then the first thing that strikes me is its determination to act, its joy in action, the assurance of being able to change things by one's own efforts. This, of course, is expressed very differently in different countries according to their various political situations and historical traditions, which in turn means according to their very different political talents. But I would like to take that up later.

Let us look briefly at the beginnings of this movement. It arose in the United States quite unexpectedly in the fifties, at the time of the so-called silent generation, the apathetic, undemonstrative generation. The immediate cause was the civil rights movement in the South, and the first to join it were students from Harvard, who then attracted students from other famous eastern universities. They went to the South, organized brilliantly, and for a time had a quite extraordinary success, so long, that is, as it was simply a question of changing the climate of opinion—which they definitely succeeded in doing in a short time—and doing away with certain laws and ordinances in the Southern states; in short, so long as it was a question of purely legal and political matters. Then they collided with the enormous social needs of the city ghettos in the North—and there they came to grief, there they could accomplish nothing.

It was only later, after they had actually accomplished what could be accomplished through purely political action, that the business with the universities began. It started in Berkeley with the Free Speech Movement and continued with the antiwar movement, and again the results have been quite extraordinary. From these beginnings and especially from these successes springs everything that has since spread around the world.

In America this new assurance that one can change things one doesn't like is conspicuous especially in small matters. A typical instance was a comparatively harmless confrontation some years ago. When students learned that the service employees of their university were not receiving standard wages, they struck—with success. Basically it was an act of solidarity with "their" university against the policy of the administration. Or, to take another instance, in 1970 university students demanded time off in order to be able to take part in the election campaign, and a number of the larger universities granted them this free time. This is a political activity *outside the university* which is made possible by the university in recognition of the fact that students are citizens as well. I consider both instances definitely positive. There are, however, other things I consider far less positive, and we will get to them later.

The basic question is: What really did happen? As I see it, for the first time in a very long while a spontaneous political movement arose which not only did not simply carry on propaganda, but acted, *and, moreover, acted almost exclusively from moral motives.* Together with this moral factor, quite rare in what is usually considered a mere power or interest play, another experience new for our time entered the game of politics: It turned out that acting is fun. This generation discovered what the eighteenth century had called "public happiness," which means that when man takes part in public life he opens up for himself a dimension of human experience

that otherwise remains closed to him and that in some way
constitutes a part of complete "happiness."

In all these matters I would rate the student movement as very positive. Its further development is another
question. How long the so-called positive factors will hold
good, whether they are not already in the process of being
dissolved, eaten away by fanaticism, ideologies, and a des-
tructiveness that often borders on the criminal on one side,
by boredom on the other, no one knows. The good things
in history are usually of very short duration, but afterward
have a decisive influence on what happens over long peri-
ods of time. Just consider how short the true classical period
in Greece was, and that we are in effect still nourished by it
today.

REIF: Ernst Bloch* recently pointed out in a lecture that the
student protest movement is not confined to its known objectives but contains principles derived from the old natural law:
"Men who do not truckle, who do not flatter the whims of
their masters." Now Bloch says that the students have brought
back into consciousness "this other subversive element of revolution," which must be distinguished from simple protest at
a bad economic situation, and in so doing have made an important contribution "to the history of revolutions and very
likely to the structure of the coming revolutions." What is
your opinion?

* German Marxist philosopher and author of the books *Natural Law
and Human Dignity* and *The Principle of Hope*. Bloch's ideas were
influential for the student protest movements of the 1960s.

ARENDT: What Ernst Bloch calls "natural law" is what I was referring to when I spoke of the conspicuous moral coloration of the movement. However, I would add—and on this point I am not in agreement with Bloch—that something similar was the case with all revolutionaries. If you look at the history of revolutions, you will see that it was never the oppressed and degraded themselves who led the way, but those who were not oppressed and not degraded but could not bear it that others were. Only, they were embarrassed to admit their moral motives—and this shame is very old. I don't want to go into the history of it here, though it has a very interesting aspect. But the moral factor has always been present, although it finds clearer expression today because people are not ashamed to own up to it.

As for the business of "not truckling," naturally it plays an especially important role in those countries, like Japan and Germany, where obsequiousness had grown to such formidable proportions, while in America, where I cannot recollect a single student ever having truckled, it is really rather meaningless. I have already mentioned that this international movement naturally takes on different national colorations, and that these colorations, simply because they are colorings, are sometimes the most striking thing; it is easy, especially for an outsider, to mistake what is most conspicuous for what is most important.

On the question of "the coming revolution" in which Ernst Bloch believes and about which I do not know whether it will come at all or what structure it might have if it did, I would like to say this: There are, it is true, a whole series of phenomena of which one can say at once that in the light of our experience (which after all is not very old, but dates only from the French and American Revolutions; before that there were rebellions and *coups d'état* but no revolutions) they belong to the prerequisites of revolution—such as the threatened breakdown of the machinery of government, its being undermined, the loss of confidence in the government on the part of the people, the failure of public services, and various others.

The loss of power and authority by all the great powers is clearly visible, even though it is accompanied by an immense accumulation of the means of violence in the hands of the governments, but the increase in weapons cannot compensate for the loss of power. Nevertheless, this situation need not lead to revolution. For one thing, it can end in counterrevolution, the establishment of dictatorships, and, for another, it can end in total anticlimax: it need not lead to anything. No one alive today knows anything about a coming revolution: "the principle of hope" [Ernst Bloch] certainly gives no sort of guarantee.

At the moment, one prerequisite for a coming revolution is lacking: a group of real revolutionaries. Just what the students on the left would most like to be—revolutionaries—that is just what they are not. Nor are they organized as revolutionaries: they have no inkling of what power means, and if power were lying in the street and they knew it was lying there, they are certainly the last to be ready to stoop down and pick it up. That is precisely what revolutionaries do. Revolutionaries do not make revolutions! The revolutionaries are those who know when power is lying in the street and when they can pick it up. Armed uprising by itself has never yet led to a revolution.

Nevertheless, what could pave the way for a revolution, in the sense of preparing the revolutionaries, is a real analysis of the existing situation such as used to be made in earlier times. To be sure, even then these analyses were mostly very inadequate, but the fact remains that they were made. In this respect I see absolutely no one, near or far, in a position to do this. The theoretical sterility and analytical dullness of this movement are just as striking and depressing as its joy in action is welcome. In Germany the movement is also rather helpless in practical matters; it can cause some rioting, but aside from the shouting of slogans it can organize nothing. In America, where on certain occasions it has brought out hundreds of thousands to demonstrate in Washington, the movement is in this respect, in its ability to act, most impressive! But the mental sterility is the same in both countries—only, in Germany, where people are so fond of loose, theoretical talk, they go about peddling obsolete conceptions and categories mainly derived from the nineteenth century, or beat you about the head with them, as the case may be. None of this bears any relationship to modern conditions. And none of this has anything to do with reflection.

Things are different, to be sure, in South America and in Eastern Europe, principally because there has been vastly more concrete practical experience there. But to examine this in detail would take us too far afield.

I would like to talk about one other point that occurred to me in connection with Ernst Bloch and "the principle of hope." The most suspicious thing about this movement in Western Europe and America is a curious despair involved in it, as though its adherents already knew they would be smashed. And as though they said to themselves: At least we want to have provoked our defeat; we do not want, in addition to everything else, to be as innocent as lambs. There is an element of running amok on the part of these bomb-throwing children. I have read that French students in Nanterre during the last disturbances—not the ones in 1968, but the recent ones—wrote on the walls: "*Ne gâchez pas votre pourriture*" ["Don't spoil your rottenness"]. Right on, right on. This conviction that everything deserves to be destroyed, that everybody deserves to go to hell—this sort of desperation can be detected everywhere, though it is less pronounced in America, where "the principle of hope" is yet unknown, perhaps because people don't yet need it so desperately.

REIF: Do you see the student protest movement in the United States as essentially frustrated?

ARENDT: By no means. The successes it has so far achieved are too great. Its success with the Negro question is spectacular, and its success in the matter of the war is perhaps even greater. It was primarily the students who succeeded in dividing the country, and ended with a majority, or at all events a very strong, highly qualified minority, against the war. It could, however, very quickly come to ruin if it actually succeeded in destroying the universities—something I consider possible. In America, perhaps this danger is less than elsewhere because American students are still more oriented towards political questions and less toward internal university problems, with the result that a part of the populace feels solidarity with them on essential matters. But in America, too, it is still conceivable that the universities will be destroyed, for the whole disturbance coincides with a crisis in the sciences, in belief in science, and in belief in progress, that is, with an internal, not simply a political, crisis of the universities.

If the students should succeed in destroying the universities, then they will have destroyed their own base of operations—and this would be true in all the countries affected, in America as well as in Europe. Nor will they be able to find another base, simply because they cannot come together anywhere else. It follows that the destruction of the universities would spell the end of the whole movement.

But it would not be the end either of the educational system or of research. Both can be organized quite differently; other forms and institutions for professional training and research are perfectly conceivable. But then there will be no more college students. Let us ask what in fact is student freedom. The universities make it possible for young people over a number of years *to stand outside all social groups and obligations*, to be truly free. If the students destroy the universities, then nothing of the sort will any longer exist; consequently there will be no rebellion against society either. In some countries and at some times, they have been well on their way to sawing off the branch they are sitting on. That in turn is connected with running amok. In this way the student protest movement could in fact not only fail to gain its demands but could also be destroyed.

REIF: Would that hold good, too, for the student protest movement in Europe?

ARENDT: Yes, it would apply to most student movements. Once more, not so much to those in South America and in the Eastern European countries, where the protest movement is not directly dependent on the universities and where a large part of the population is behind it.

REIF: In your study *On Violence*, there is this sentence: "The third world is not a reality but an ideology." That sounds like blasphemy. For, of course, the third world is a reality; what's more, a reality that was brought into being first by the Western colonial powers and later with the cooperation of the United States. And so it is not at all surprising that this reality produced by capitalism should result, under the influence of the worldwide and general indignation of youth, in a new ideology. However, the significant thing, I believe, is not this ideology of the New Left, but simply the existence of the third world, the reality of the third world, which first made this ideology possible.

Do you really intend by your astonishing sentence to question the reality of the third world as such? Possibly there's a misunderstanding here that you could clear up.

ARENDT: Not a bit of it. I am truly of the opinion that the third world is exactly what I said, an ideology or an illusion.

Africa, Asia, South America—those are realities. If you now compare these regions with Europe and America, then you can say of them—but only from this perspective—that they are underdeveloped, and you assert thereby that this is a crucial common denominator between these countries. However, you overlook the innumerable things they do *not* have in common, and the fact that what they do have in common is only a contrast that exists with another world; which means that the idea of underdevelopment as the important factor is a European American prejudice. The whole thing is simply a question of perspective; there is a logical fallacy here. Try telling a Chinese sometime that he belongs to exactly the same world as an African Bantu tribesman and, believe me, you'll get the surprise of your life. The only ones who have an obviously political interest in saying that there is a third world are, of course, those who stand on the lowest step—that is, the Negroes in Africa. In their case it's easy to understand; all the rest is empty talk.

The New Left has borrowed the catchword of the third world from the arsenal of the Old Left. It has been taken in by the distinction made by the imperialists between colonial countries and colonizing powers. For the imperialists, Egypt was, naturally, like India: they both fell under the heading of "subject races." This imperialist leveling out of all differences is copied by the New Left, only with labels reversed. It is always the same old story: being taken in by every catchword, the inability to think or else the unwillingness to see phenomena as they really are, without applying categories to them in the belief that they can thereby be classified. It is just this that constitutes theoretical helplessness.

The new slogan—Natives of all colonies or of all former colonies or of all underdeveloped countries unite!—is even crazier than the old one from which it was copied: Workers of the world unite!—which, after all, has been thoroughly discredited. I am certainly not of the opinion that one can learn very much from history—for history constantly confronts us with what is new—but there are a couple of small things that it should be possible to learn. What fills me with such misgivings is that I do not see anywhere people of this generation recognizing realities as such, and taking the trouble to think about them.

REIF: Marxist philosophers and historians, and not just those in the strict sense of the word, today take the view that in this stage of the historical development of mankind there are only two possible alternatives for the future: capitalism or socialism. In your view, does another alternative exist?

ARENDT: I see no such alternatives in history; nor do I know what is in store there. Let's not talk about such grand matters as "the historical development of mankind"—in all likelihood it will take a turn that corresponds neither to the one nor to the other, and let us hope it will come as a surprise to us.

But let's look at your alternatives historically for a moment: it began, after all, with capitalism, an economic system that no one had planned and no one had foreseen. This system, as is generally known, owed its start to a monstrous process of expropriation such as has never occurred before in history in this form—that is, without military conquest. Expropriation, the initial accumulation of capital—that was the law according to which capitalism arose and according to which it has advanced step by step. Now just what people imagine by socialism I do not know. But if you look at what has actually happened in Russia, then you can see that there the process of expropriation has been carried further; and you can observe that something very similar is going on in the

modern capitalist countries, where it is as though the old ex
propriation process is again let loose. Overtaxation, a *de facto*
devaluation of currency, inflation coupled with a recession—
what else are these but relatively mild forms of expropriation?
Only in the Western countries are there political and
legal obstacles that constantly keep this process of expropriation from reaching the point where life would be completely
unbearable. In Russia there is, of course, not socialism, but
state socialism, which is the same thing as state capitalism
would be—that is, total expropriation. Total expropriation
occurs when all political and legal safeguards of private ownership have disappeared. In Russia, for instance, certain groups
enjoy a very high standard of living. The trouble is only that
whatever these people may have at their disposition—cars,
country houses, expensive furniture, chauffeur-driven lim-
ousines, et cetera—they do not own; it can be taken away
from them by the government any day. No man there is so
rich that he cannot be made a beggar overnight—without
even the right to employment—in case of any conflict with
the ruling powers. (One glance into recent Soviet literature,
where people have started to tell the truth, will testify to the
atrocious consequences more tellingly than all economic and
political theories.)

All our experiences—as distinguished from theories and
ideologies—tell us that the process of expropriation, which
started with the rise of capitalism, does not stop with the
expropriation of the means of production; only legal and
political institutions that are independent of the economic
forces and their automatism can control and check the inher-
ently monstrous potentialities of this process. Such political

controls seem to function best in the so-called welfare states whether they call themselves socialist or capitalist. What protects freedom is the division between governmental and economic power, or, to put it into Marxian language, the fact that the state and its constitution are not superstructures. What protects us in the so-called capitalist countries of the West is not capitalism, but a legal system that prevents the daydreams of big-business management of trespassing into the private sphere of its employees from coming true. But this dream does come true wherever the government itself becomes the employer. It is no secret that the clearance system for American government employees does not respect private life; the recent appetite of certain governmental agencies to bug private homes could also be seen as an attempt on the part of the government to treat all citizens as prospective government employees. And what else is bugging but a form of expropriation? The government agency establishes itself as a kind of co-owner of the apartments and houses of citizens. In Russia no fancy gadgets in the walls are necessary; there, a spy sits in every citizen's apartment anyhow.

If I were to judge these developments from a Marxian viewpoint, I would say: Perhaps expropriation is indeed in the very nature of modern production, and socialism is, as Marx believed, nothing but the inevitable result of industrial society as it was started by capitalism. Then the question is what we can do to get and keep this process under control so that it does not degenerate, under one name or another, into the monstrosities in which it has fallen in the East. In certain so-called communist countries—in Yugoslavia, for instance, but even in East Germany—there are attempts to decontrol and decentralize the economy, and very substantial concessions are being made in order to prevent the most horrifying consequences of the expropriation process, which, fortunately enough, also has turned out to be very unsatisfactory for production once a certain point of centralization and enslavement of the workers has been reached.

Fundamentally it is a question of how much property and how many rights we can allow a person to possess even under the very inhuman conditions of much of modern economy. But nobody can tell me that there is such a thing as workers "owning their factories." Collective ownership is, if you reflect for a second, a contradiction in terms. Property is what belongs to me; ownership relates to what is my own by definition. Other people's means of production should not, of course, belong to me; they might perhaps be controlled by a third authority, which means they belong to no one. The worst possible owner would be the government, unless its powers in this economic sphere are strictly controlled and checked by a truly independent judiciary. Our problem today is not how to expropriate the expropriators, but, rather, how to arrange matters so that the masses, dispossessed by industrial society in capitalist and socialist systems, can regain property. For this reason alone, the alternative between capitalism and socialism is false—not only because neither exists anywhere in its pure state anyhow, but because we have here twins, each wearing a different hat.

The same state of affairs can be looked at from a different perspective—from that of the oppressed themselves—which does not make the result any better. In that case one must say that capitalism has destroyed the estates, the corporations, the guilds, the whole structure of feudal society. It has done away with all the collective groups which were a protection for the individual and for his property, which guaranteed him a certain security, though not, of course, complete safety. In their place it has put the "classes," essentially just two: the exploiters and the exploited. Now the working class, simply because it was a class and a collective, still provided the individual with a certain protection, and later, when it learned to organize, it fought for and secured considerable rights for itself. The chief distinction today is not between socialist and capitalist countries but between countries that respect these rights, as, for instance, Sweden on one side, the United States on the other, and those that do not, as, for instance, Franco's Spain on one side, Soviet Russia on the other.

What, then, has socialism or communism, taken in its pure form, done? It has destroyed this class, too, its institutions, the unions and the labor parties, and its rights—collective bargaining, strikes, unemployment insurance, social security. In their stead, these regimes offered the illusion that the factories were the property of the working class, which as a class had just been abolished, and the atrocious lie that unemployment no longer existed, a lie based on nothing but the very real nonexistence of unemployment insurance. In essence, socialism has simply continued, and driven to its extreme, what capitalism began. Why should it be the remedy?

REIF: Marxist intellectuals often emphasize that socialism, in spite of alienation, is always capable of regeneration through its own strength. As an ideal example of this regeneration there is the Czechoslovakian model of democratic socialism.

In view of the increase in military weapons by the Soviet Union and Soviet hegemony in other areas as well, how
do you judge the chances of a new initiative for democratic
socialism in the East, oriented in the spirit of the Czechoslovakian or Yugoslavian models?

ARENDT: What you just said in your first sentence really
shocked me. To call Stalin's rule an "alienation" seems to me
a euphemism used to sweep under the rug not only facts, but
the most hair-raising crimes as well. I say this to you simply to
call your attention to how very much this jargon has already
twisted the facts: to call something "alienation"—that is no
less than a crime.

Now so far as economic systems and "models" are concerned, in time something will emerge from all the experimentation here and there if the great powers leave the small
countries in peace. What that will be we cannot of course tell
in a field so dependent on practice as economics. However,
there will be experimentation first of all with the problem of
ownership. On the basis of the very scanty information at my
disposal, I would say that this is already happening in East
Germany and in Yugoslavia with interesting results.

In East Germany, a kind of cooperative system, which
does not derive at all from socialism and which has proved
its worth in Denmark and in Israel, has been built into the
"socialistic" economic system—thereby making it work. In
Yugoslavia we have the "system of self-management" in the
factories, a new version of the old "workers' councils," which,
incidentally, also never became part of orthodox socialist
or communist doctrine—despite Lenin's "all power to the

Soviets." (The councils, the only true outgrowth of the revolutions themselves as distinguished from revolutionary parties and ideologies, have been mercilessly destroyed precisely by the Communist Party and by Lenin himself.)

None of these experiments redefines legitimate property in a satisfactory way, but they may be steps in this direction—the East German cooperatives by combining private ownership with the need for joint property in the means of production and distribution, the workers' councils by providing job security instead of the security of private property. In both instances individual workers are no longer atomized but belong to a new collective, the cooperative or the factory's council, as a kind of compensation for membership in a class.

You ask also about the experiments and reforms. These have nothing to do with economic systems—except that the economic system should not be used to deprive people of their freedom. This is done when a dissenter or opponent becomes "unemployable" or when consumer goods are so scarce and life so uncomfortable that it is easy for the government to "buy" whole sections of the population. What people in the East do care about are freedom, civil rights, legal guarantees. For these are the conditions for being free to say, to write, and to print whatever one likes. The Soviet Union marched into Czechoslovakia not because of the new "economic model" but because of the *political* reforms connected with it. It did not march into East Germany, although today people there, as in other satellite countries, live better than in the Soviet Union and perhaps soon will live just as well and eventually even better than those in West Germany. And then the difference will be "only" that in one country people can say and, within limits, also do what they like and in the other they cannot. Believe me, *that* makes an enormous difference to everyone.

The Soviet Union has an interest in striking home wherever these economic experiments are joined to a struggle for freedom. Without doubt this was the case in Czechoslovakia. It is not the case in East Germany; therefore the German Democratic Republic is left in peace. Under Ulbricht's rule,* the German Democratic Republic has become constantly more tyrannical ideologically the greater its economic concessions.

The Soviet Union must also strike home whenever it fears that one of the satellite countries is breaking away from the Warsaw Pact. Whether this fear, certainly present, was justified in the case of Czechoslovakia I do not know, but I consider it possible. On the other hand, I do not believe that the Soviet Union will intervene militarily in Yugoslavia. It would encounter there a very considerable military opposition, and it cannot today afford this kind of confrontation. It is not that firmly seated in the saddle, being a great power.

REIF: Do you give socialism as the dominant conception at present for the future of human society any chance of realization?

ARENDT: This naturally brings up the question again of what socialism really is. Even Marx hardly knew what he should concretely picture by that.

---

* Walter Ulbricht, first secretary of the Socialist Unity Party and de facto leader of East Germany from 1950 to 1971.

REIF: If I may interrupt: what is meant is socialism, as I said before, oriented in the spirit of the Czechoslovakian or Yugoslavian model.

ARENDT: You mean, then, what today is called "socialistic humanism." This new slogan means no more than the attempt to undo the inhumanity brought about by socialism without reintroducing a so-called capitalist system, although the clear tendency in Yugoslavia towards an open market economy could very easily, and almost certainly will, be so interpreted, not only by the Soviet Union, but by all true believers.

Generally speaking, I would say that I grant a chance to all the small countries that want to experiment, whether they call themselves socialist or not, but I am very skeptical about the great powers. These mass societies can no longer be controlled, let alone governed. The Czechoslovakian and Yugoslavian models, if you take these two as examples, naturally have a chance. I would also include perhaps Romania, perhaps Hungary, where the revolution did not by any means end catastrophically, as it might have ended under Stalin—simply with the deportation of 50 percent of the population. In all these countries something is going on, and it will be very hard to reverse their reform efforts, their attempts to escape from the worst consequences of dictatorship and to solve their economic problems independently and sensibly.

There is another factor we should take into account. The Soviet Union and, in various degrees, its satellite states are not nation-states, but are composed of nationalities. In each of them, the dictatorship is more or less in the hands of the dominant nationality, and the opposition against it always risks turning into a national liberation movement. This is especially true in the Soviet Union, where the Russian dictators always live in the fear of a collapse of the Russian empire— and not just a change of government.

This concern has nothing to do with socialism; it is, and always has been, an issue of sheer power politics. I don't think that the Soviet Union would have proceeded as it did in Czechoslovakia if it had not been worried about its own inner opposition, not only the opposition of the intellectuals, but the latent opposition of its own nationalities. One should not forget that during the Prague Spring the government granted considerable concessions to the Slovaks which only recently, certainly under Russian influence, were canceled. All attempts at decentralization are feared by Moscow. A new model—this means, to the Russians, not only a more humane handling of the economic or intellectual questions but also the threat of the decomposition of the Russian empire.

REIF: I think the Soviet leaders' fear, specifically of the opposition of the intellectuals, plays a special role. After all, it is an opposition that today is making itself felt in a wider field. There is even a civil rights movement on the part of young intellectuals which operates with all available legal and, needless to say, also illegal means, such as underground newspapers, et cetera.

ARENDT: Yes, I am aware of that. And the leaders of the Soviet Union are naturally very much afraid of it. They are very much afraid that if the success of this movement extends to the people, as distinguished from the intellectuals, it could mean that the Ukrainians would once more want to have a state of their own, likewise the Tartars, who in any case were so abominably treated, and so on. Therefore the rulers of the Soviet Union are on an even shakier footing than the rulers in the satellite countries. But you see, too, that Tito in Yugoslavia is afraid of the problem of nationalities and not at all of so-called capitalism.

REIF: How do you account for the fact that the reform movement in the East—I am thinking not only of the much-cited Czechoslovakian model, but also of various publications by Soviet intellectuals advocating democratization of the Soviet Union, and similar protests—never put forward any form of capitalism, however modified, as an alternative to the system they are criticizing.

ARENDT: Well, I could say to you that these people are obviously of my opinion, that just as socialism is no remedy for capitalism, capitalism cannot be a remedy or an alternative for socialism. But I will not harp on that. The contest is never simply over an economic system. The economic system is involved only so far as a dictatorship hinders the economy from developing as productively as it would without dictatorial constraint. For the rest, it has to do with the political question: It has to do with what kind of state one wants to have, what kind of constitution, what kind of legislation, what sort of safeguards for the freedom of the spoken and printed word; that is, it has to do with what our innocent children in the West call "bourgeois freedom."

There is no such thing; freedom is freedom whether

guaranteed by the laws of a "bourgeois" government or a "communist" state. From the fact that communist governments today do not respect civil rights and do not guarantee freedom of speech and association it does not follow that such rights and freedoms are "bourgeois." "Bourgeois freedom" is frequently and quite wrongly equated with the freedom to make more money than one actually needs. For this is the only "freedom" which the East, where in fact one can become extremely rich, respects, too. The contrast between rich and poor—if we are to talk a sensible language for once and not jargon—in respect to income is greater in the East than in most other countries, greater even than in the United States if you disregard a few thousand multimillionaires.

But that is not the point either. I repeat: The point is simply and singly whether I can say and print what I wish, or whether I cannot; whether my neighbors spy on me or don't. Freedom always implies freedom of dissent. No ruler before Stalin and Hitler contested the freedom to say yes—Hitler excluding Jews and gypsies from the right to consent and Stalin having been the only dictator who chopped off the heads of his most enthusiastic supporters, perhaps because he figured that whoever says yes can also say no. No tyrant before them went that far—and that did not pay off either.

None of these systems, not even that of the Soviet Union, is still truly totalitarian—though I have to admit that I am not in a position to judge China. At present only the people who dissent and are in the opposition are excluded, but this does not signify by any means that there is any freedom there. And it is precisely in political freedom and assured basic rights that the opposition forces are interested—and rightly so.

REIF: How do you stand on Thomas Mann's statement "Anti-Bolshevism is the basic foolishness of our time"?

ARENDT: There are so many absurdities in our time that it is hard to assign first place. But, to speak seriously, anti-Bolshevism as a theory, as an ism, is the invention of the ex-communists. By that I do not mean just any former Bolsheviks or communists, but, rather, those who "*believed*" and then one day were personally disillusioned by Mr. Stalin; that is, people who were not really revolutionaries or politically engaged but who, as they themselves said, had lost a god and then went in search of a new god and also the opposite, a new devil. They simply reversed the pattern.

But to say that the mentality of these people changed, that instead of searching for beliefs they saw realities, took them into account, and attempted to change things is erroneous. Whether anti-Bolshevists announce that the East is the Devil, or Bolshevists maintain that America is the Devil, as far as their habits of thought go it amounts to the same thing. The mentality is still the same. It sees only black and white. In reality there is no such thing. If one does not know the whole spectrum of political colors of an epoch, cannot distinguish between the basic conditions of the different countries, the various stages of development, traditions, kinds and grades in production, technology, mentality, and so on, then one simply does not know how to move and take one's bearings in this field. One can do nothing but smash the world to bits in order finally to have before one's eyes one thing: plain black.

REIF: At the end of *On Violence*, you write that we know "or should know that every decrease of power is an open invitation to violence—if only because those who hold power and feel it slipping from their hands ... have always found it difficult to resist the temptation to substitute violence for it." What does this weighty sentence mean in respect to the present political situation in the United States?

ARENDT: I spoke earlier about the loss of power on the part of the great powers. If we consider this concretely, what does it mean? In all republics with representative governments, power resides in the people. That means that the people empower certain individuals to represent them, to act in their name. When we talk about loss of power, that signifies that the people have withdrawn their consent from what their representatives, the empowered elected officials, do.

Those who have been empowered naturally feel powerful; even when the people withdraw the basis of that power, the feeling of power remains. That is the situation in America— not only there, to be sure. This state of affairs, incidentally, has nothing to do with the fact that the people are divided, but, rather, is to be explained by loss of confidence in the so-called system. In order to maintain the system, the empowered ones begin to act as rulers and resort to force. They substitute force for the assent of the people; that is the turning point.

How does this stand in America at present? The matter can be illustrated by various examples, but I would like to elucidate it chiefly by the war in Vietnam, which not only actually divides the people in the United States but, even more important, has caused a loss of confidence and thereby a loss of power. To be specific, it has produced the "credibility gap," which means that those in power are no longer believed—quite apart from whether one agrees with them or not. I know that in Europe politicians never have been believed, that, indeed, people are of the opinion that politicians must and should lie as part of their trade. But that was not the case in America.

Naturally, there have always been state secrets which on specific grounds of practical politics needed to be strictly guarded. Often the truth was not told; but neither were direct lies. Now, as you know, the Gulf of Tonkin resolution, which gave the president a free hand in an undeclared war, was forced through Congress on the basis of a provably inaccurate presentation of the circumstances. This affair cost Johnson the presidency; also, the bitterness of the opposition in the Senate can hardly be explained without it. Since that time, among widening circles, the Vietnam War has been considered illegal—not only peculiarly inhuman, not only immoral, but *illegal*. In America that has a different weight than in Europe.

REIF: And yet among American labor there is very strong agitation *for* the engagement of the United States in Vietnam. How is that to be explained in this connection?

ARENDT: The first impetus of opposition to the war came from the universities, especially from the student body, that is, from the same groups that were engaged in the civil rights movement. This opposition was directed from the beginning against the so-called system, whose most loyal supporters today are unquestionably to be found among the workers, that is, in the lower-income groups. (On Wall Street the so-called capitalists demonstrated against the government and the construction workers for it.) In this, the decisive part was played not so much by the question of the war as by the color problem.

It has turned out that in the eastern and northern parts of the country integration of the Negroes into the higher-income groups encounters no very serious or insuperable difficulties. Today everywhere it is really a *fait accompli*. Dwellings with relatively high rentals can be integrated if the black tenants belong to the same upper level as the white or yellow (especially the Chinese, who are everywhere especially favored as neighbors). Since the number of successful black businessmen is very small, this really applies to the academic and liberal professions—doctors, lawyers, professors, actors, writers, and so on.

The same integration in the middle and lower levels of the middle class, and especially among the workers who in respect to income belong to the upper level of the lower middle class, leads to catastrophe, and this indeed not only because the lower middle class happens to be particularly "reactionary," but because these classes believe, not without reason, that all these reforms relating to the Negro problem are being carried out at their expense. This can best be illustrated by the example of the schools. Public schools in America, including high schools, are free. The better these schools are, the greater are the chances for children without means to get into the colleges and universities, that is, to improve their social position. In the big cities this public school system, under the weight of a very numerous, almost exclusively black *Lumpenproletariat*, has with very few exceptions broken down; these institutions, in which children are kept for twelve years without even learning to read and write, can hardly be described as schools. Now if a section of the city becomes black as a result of the policy of integration, then the streets run to seed, the schools are neglected, the children run wild—in short, the neighborhood very quickly becomes a slum. The principal sufferers, aside from the blacks themselves, are the Italians, the Irish, the Poles, and other ethnic groups who are not poor but are not rich enough either to be able simply to move away or to send their children to the very expensive private schools.

This, however, is perfectly possible for the upper classes, though often at the cost of considerable sacrifice. People are perfectly right in saying that soon in New York only the very poor and the very rich will be able to live. Almost all the white residents who can do so send their children either to private schools, which are often very good, or to the principally Catholic denominational schools. Negroes belonging to the upper levels can also do this. The working class cannot, nor can the lower middle class. What makes these people especially bitter is that the middle-class liberals have put through laws whose consequences they do not feel. They demand integration of the public schools, elimination of neighborhood schools (black children, who in large measure are simply left to neglect, are transported in buses out of the slums into schools in predominantly white neighborhoods), forced integration of neighborhoods—and send their own children to private schools and move to the suburbs, something that only those at a certain income level can afford.

To this another factor is added, which is present in other countries as well. Marx may have said that the proletarian has no country; it is well known that the proletarians have never shared this point of view. The lower social classes are especially susceptible to nationalism, chauvinism, and imperialistic policies. One serious split in the civil rights movement into "black" and "white" came as a result of the war question: the white students coming from good middle-class homes at once joined the opposition, in contrast to the Negroes, whose leaders were very slow in making up their minds to demonstrate against the war in Vietnam. This was true even of Martin Luther King. The fact that the army gives the lower social classes certain opportunities for education and vocational training naturally also plays a role here.

REIF: You reproach the New Left in West Germany with, among other things, having never "concerned itself seriously with the recognition of the Oder-Neisse Line,* which, after all, is one of the crucial issues of German foreign policy and has been the touchstone of German nationalism ever since the defeat of the Hitler regime." I doubt that your thesis can be maintained in this uncompromising form, for the German New Left is also urging the recognition, not only of the

---

* At the time of this interview, the Oder-Neisse Line was the border between the German Democratic Republic and Poland. It was established by the Potsdam Agreement of 1945 between the United States, the United Kingdom, and the Soviet Union, which resulted in Poland encompassing territories that, before the war, had been part of Germany. West German politicians refused to recognize the Oder-Neisse Line until 1970, though East Germany had confirmed it in 1950.

Oder-Neisse Line by Bonn, but of the German Democratic Republic as well. However, the New Left is isolated from the general population, and it is not within its power to give practical political reality to such theoretical demands. But even if the numerically extremely weak New Left were to intervene "seriously" for the recognition of the Oder-Neisse Line would German nationalism thereby suffer a decisive defeat?

ARENDT: As far as practical political consequences are concerned, a change of policies in Persia* was certainly even less likely. The trouble with the New Left is that it obviously cares about nothing less than eventual consequences of its demonstrations. In contrast to the shah of Persia, the Oder-Neisse Line is a matter of direct responsibility for every German citizen; to demonstrate for its recognition and to go on record on this issue make sense regardless of practical political consequences. It proves nothing whatsoever if the New Left comes out "also" for the recognition of the new boundary with Poland—as many good liberal Germans have done. The point is that this issue has never been at the center of their propaganda, which means simply that they dodge all matters that are real and involve direct responsibility. This is true of their theories as well as of their practices.

There are two possible explanations for this shirking of an eminently practical issue. I have so far mentioned only German nationalism, of which, all rhetoric to the contrary

---

* Arendt is referring here to the increasingly autocratic policies of Shah Mohammed Reza Pahlavi. When the shah traveled to Germany on an official visit in 1967, German students demonstrated against what they saw as their government's complicity with an oppressive regime.

notwithstanding, one might also suspect the New Left. The second possibility would be that this movement in its German version has indulged in so much high-flown theoretical nonsense that it cannot see what is in front of its nose. This seems to have been the case at the time of the *Notstandsgesetze.*[*] You remember how late the student movement was in becoming aware that something of considerable importance was happening in Parliament, certainly of greater importance for Germany than the visit of oriental potentates.

When the American students demonstrate against the war in Vietnam, they are demonstrating against a policy of immediate interest to their country and to themselves. When the German students do the same, it is pretty much as with the shah of Persia; there is not the slightest possibility of their being personally held to account. Passionate interest in international affairs in which no risk and no responsibility are involved has often been a cloak to hide down-to-earth national interests; in politics, idealism is frequently no more than an excuse for not recognizing unpleasant realities. Idealism can be a form of evading reality altogether, and this, I think, is much more likely the case here. The New Left simply overlooked the issue, and that means it overlooked the single moral question that, in postwar Germany, was still really open and subject to debate. And it also overlooked one of the few decisive international political issues in which Germany would have been able to play a significant role after the end of World War II. The failure of the German government, especially

---

[*] The *Notstandsgesetze*—Emergency Laws—were passed in West Germany in May 1968. They allowed the government to curtail some constitutional rights during a crisis.

under Adenauer,* to recognize the Oder-Neisse Line in time has contributed a great deal to the consolidation of the Soviet satellite system. It ought to be perfectly clear to everyone that fear of Germany on the part of the satellite nations has decisively slowed down, and in part rendered impossible, all reform movements in Eastern Europe. The fact that not even the Left, New or Old, dared to touch this most sensitive point of postwar Germany could only strengthen considerably this fear.

REIF: To come back once more to your study *On Violence:* in it (that is, in its German version) you write: "So long as national independence, namely, freedom from foreign rule, and the sovereignty of the state, namely, the claim to unchecked and unlimited power in foreign affairs, are identified—and no revolution has thus far been able to shake this state concept—not even a theoretical solution of the problem of war, on which depends not so much the future of mankind as the question of whether mankind will have a future, is so much as conceivable, and a guaranteed peace on earth is as utopian as the squaring of the circle." What other conception of the state do you have in mind?

ARENDT: What I have in mind is not so much a different state concept as the necessity of changing this one. What we call the "state" is not much older than the fifteenth and sixteenth centuries, and the same thing is true of the concept of sovereignty. Sovereignty means, among other things, that conflicts

* Konrad Adenauer, chancellor of West Germany from 1949 to 1963.

of an international character can ultimately be settled only by war; there is no other last resort. Today, however, war—quite apart from all pacifist considerations—among the great powers has become impossible owing to the monstrous development of the means of violence. And so the question arises: What is to take the place of this last resort?

War has, so to speak, become a luxury which only the small nations can still afford, and they only so long as they are not drawn into the spheres of influence of the great powers and do not possess nuclear weapons themselves. The great powers interfere in these wars in part because they are obliged to defend their clients and in part because this has become an important piece of the strategy of mutual deterrence on which the peace of the world today rests.

Between sovereign states there can be no last resort except war; if war no longer serves that purpose, that fact alone proves that we must have a new concept of the state. This new concept of the state, to be sure, will not result from the founding of a new international court that would function better than the one at The Hague, or a new League of Nations, since the same conflicts between sovereign or ostensibly sovereign governments can only be played out there all over again—on the level of discourse, to be sure, which is more important than is usually thought.

The mere rudiments I see for a new state concept can be found in the federal system, whose advantage it is that power moves neither from above nor from below, but is horizontally directed so that the federated units mutually check and control their powers. For the real difficulty in speculating on these matters is that the final resort should not be *super*national but *inter*national. A supernational authority would either be ineffective or be monopolized by the nation that happens to be the strongest, and so would lead to world government, which could easily become the most frightful tyranny conceivable, since from its global police force there would be no escape—until it finally fell apart.

Where do we find models that could help us in construing, at least theoretically, an *inter*national authority as the highest control agency? This sounds like a paradox, since what is highest cannot well be in between, but it is nevertheless the real question. When I said that none of the revolutions, each of which overthrew one form of government and replaced it with another, had been able to shake the state concept and its sovereignty, I had in mind something that I tried to elaborate a bit in my book *On Revolution*.* Since the revolutions of the eighteenth century, every large upheaval has actually developed the rudiments of an entirely new form of government, which emerged independent of all preceding revolutionary theories, directly out of the course of the revolution itself, that is, out of the experiences of action and out of the resulting will of the actors to participate in the further development of public affairs.

This new form of government is the council system, which, as we know, has perished every time and everywhere, destroyed either directly by the bureaucracy of the nation-states or by the party machines. Whether this system is a pure utopia—in any case it would be a people's utopia, not the utopia of theoreticians and ideologies—I cannot say. It seems

* *On Revolution* (New York: Viking Press, 1963).

to me, however, the single alternative that has ever appeared in history, and has reappeared time and again. Spontaneous organization of council systems occurred in all revolutions, in the French Revolution, with Jefferson in the American Revolution, in the Parisian commune, in the Russian revolutions, in the wake of the revolutions in Germany and Austria at the end of World War I, finally in the Hungarian Revolution. What is more, they never came into being as a result of a conscious revolutionary tradition or theory, but entirely spontaneously, each time as though there had never been anything of the sort before. Hence the council system seems to correspond to and to spring from the very experience of political action.

In this direction, I think, there must be something to be found, a completely different principle of organization, which begins from below, continues upward, and finally leads to a parliament. But we can't talk about that now. And it is not necessary, since important studies on this subject have been published in recent years in France and Germany, and anyone seriously interested can inform himself.

To prevent a misunderstanding that might easily occur today, I must say that the communes of hippies and dropouts have nothing to do with this. On the contrary, a renunciation of the whole of public life, of politics in general, is at their foundation; they are refuges for people who have suffered political shipwreck—and as such they are completely justified on personal grounds. I find the forms of these communes very often grotesque—in Germany as well as in America—but I understand them and have nothing against them. Politically they are meaningless. The councils desire the exact opposite, even if they begin very small—as neighborhood councils, professional councils, councils within factories, apartment houses, and so on. There are, indeed, councils of the most various kinds, by no means only workers' councils; workers' councils are a special case in this field.

The councils say: We want to participate, we want to debate, we want to make our voices heard in public, and we want to have a possibility to determine the political course of our country. Since the country is too big for all of us to come together and determine our fate, we need a number of public spaces within it. The booth in which we deposit our ballots is unquestionably too small, for this booth has room for only one. The parties are completely unsuitable; there we are, most of us, nothing but the manipulated electorate. But if only ten of us are sitting around a table, each expressing his opinion, each hearing the opinions of others, then a rational formation of opinion can take place through the exchange of opinions. There, too, it will become clear which one of us is best suited to present our view before the next higher council, where in turn our view will be clarified through the influence of other views, revised, or proved wrong.

By no means does every resident of a country need to be a member of such councils. Not everyone wants to or has to concern himself with public affairs. In this fashion a self-selective process is possible that would draw together a true political elite in a country. Anyone who is not interested in public affairs will simply have to be satisfied with their being decided without him. But each person must be given the opportunity.

In this direction I see the possibility of forming a new

concept of the state. A council-state of this sort, to which the principle of sovereignty would be wholly alien, would be admirably suited to federations of the most various kinds, especially because in it power would be constituted horizontally and not vertically. But if you ask me now what prospect it has of being realized, then I must say to you: Very slight, if at all. And yet perhaps, after all—in the wake of the next revolution.

THE LAST INTERVIEW

INTERVIEW BY ROGER ERRERA
UN CERTAIN REGARD, ORTF TV, FRANCE
OCTOBER 1973

TRANSLATED BY ANDREW BROWN

In October 1973, Hannah Arendt was interviewed by Roger Errera for the Office de Radiodiffusion-Télévision Française (ORTF). Recorded over several days, the interviews were later worked into a fifty-minute television feature directed by Jean-Claude Lubtchansky for the series *Un certain regard*, and first broadcast on July 6, 1974.

For the film, Arendt's answers were translated into French and dubbed, with Arendt's original voice behind it. By using this soundtrack and various transcripts and translations of the interviews, Arendt scholar Ursula Ludz reconstructed Arendt's original answers and assembled an authoritative manuscript of the interview as it was televised. Stars indicate places where there was a cut in the film and where different sessions of the interviews have been pieced together.

Roger Errera's questions have been translated from French for this publication. Arendt occasionally replied in a mixture of German, French, and English—her responses in French have been left, with translations in brackets where deemed necessary. Though the other interviews in this collection were edited before their original publication, and Arendt's general practice was to go over anything she wrote in English with a friend or editor to fix her mistakes, this interview has been only lightly edited to correct some grammatical mistakes and eliminate repetitions. Arendt's unique style of English and the conversational tone of the interview have been respected.

INTERVIEWING HANNAH ARENDT
BY ROGER ERRERA

What follows is the text of my filmed interview with Hannah
Arendt, which took place in New York in October 1973. My
own interest in Arendt's work began in 1965. I had reviewed
the French translations of *Eichmann in Jerusalem*, *On Revolution*, and *The Origins of Totalitarianism*, and I published
French translations of *Antisemitism* and *Crises of the Republic* in the Diaspora series at Calmann-Lévy in 1972 and 1973.
I had also met Arendt several times, first at her apartment
in New York in the winter of 1967, then in Cologne in
1972, and near Ascona in Switzerland, when she stayed
in Tegna.

The initiative for the film came from a good friend, the
late Pierre Schaeffer, then head of the Research Service of
ORTF (French public radio and television). He asked me
whether I would be interested. My answer was yes, while Arendt's was, first, a categorical no. She later accepted. The fact
that we had met earlier no doubt helped.

In October 1973, we went to New York. I had spent the
summer in Greece reading her books again and preparing the
interview. I sent her a short list of topics, which was accepted.
We agreed on the procedure: two hours of interviewing every
day, over several days, in a rental place, a TV studio or at
the office of her publisher (Harcourt Brace Jovanovich). She
strongly refused to be filmed at home.

The moment was not exactly a calm one, politically
speaking. In the Middle East, the October War had just taken
place. In the United States, the Watergate affair had begun.

It would lead to the resignation of President Nixon in August 1974, under the threat of impeachment. If I remember well, we learned, in the course of our talks, of the dismissal of Archibald Cox, then special prosecutor, and the resignation of Elliot Richardson, then attorney general.

There is more than an echo of these events in the interview. During it, Hannah Arendt was extremely courteous and attentive, fully controlled, at times consulting a few notes (for quotations). It seems to me that she said exactly what she meant to say, correcting herself immediately whenever necessary. No anecdotes, no small talk. With a permanent grace she accepted what was for her neither a familiar nor a relaxing exercise.

Many themes were discussed by us: Europe and the United States; the pending constitutional crisis in Washington; the legacy of the sixties and early seventies in the American polity; the uniqueness of totalitarianism in the twentieth century; Israel, the Diaspora, and the Jewish condition. We could have spent hours, even days on each of them. It was a rare privilege for me to see and listen to her thinking aloud.

For several months after the filming, I worked with J.-C. Lubtchansky to assemble the parts of the film and make a whole out of them for the fifty-minute program. The film was broadcast in the spring of 1974.

A year later, I met Hannah Arendt again in New York, in the fall of 1975, shortly before she died on December 4. When, that same day, I learned of her death, I spent the whole night writing an obituary for her which appeared in *Le Monde* the next day—as a postface to our interrupted dialogue.

ARENDT: I may need a glass of water, if I could have that.

ERRERA: You arrived in this country in 1941. You'd come from Europe, and you've been living here for thirty-two years. When you arrived from Europe, what was your main impression?

ARENDT: *Ma impression dominante*, well, *mon impression dominante* . . . Well. See, this is not a nation-state, America is not a nation-state and Europeans have a hell of a time understanding this simple fact, which, after all, they could know theoretically; it is, this country is united neither by heritage, nor by memory, nor by soil, nor by language, nor by origin from the same . . . There are no natives here. The natives were the Indians. Everyone else is a citizen and these citizens are united only by one thing, and that's a lot: that is, you become a citizen of the United States by simple consent to the Constitution. The constitution—that is a scrap of paper, according to French as well as German common opinion, and you can change it. No, here it is a sacred document, it is the constant remembrance of one sacred act, and that is the act of foundation. And the foundation is to make a union out of wholly disparate ethnic minorities and regions, and still (a) have a union and (b) not assimilate or level down these differences. And all this is very difficult to understand for a foreigner. It's what a foreigner never understands. We can say this is a government by law and not by men. To what extent that is true, and needs to be true for the well-being of the country . . . I almost said, the nation—but for the well-being of the country, for the United States of America, for the republic, really . . .

ERRERA: Over the last ten years, America has experienced a wave of political violence marked by the assassination of the president and his brother, by the Vietnam War, by the Watergate affair. Why can America overcome crises that in Europe have led to changes of government, or even to very serious domestic unrest?

ARENDT: Now let me try it a little differently. I think the turning point in this whole business was indeed the assassination of the president. No matter how you explain it and no matter what you know or don't know about it, it was quite clear that now, really for the first time in a very long time in American history, a direct crime had interfered with the political process. And this somehow has changed the political process. You know, other assassinations followed, Bobby Kennedy, Martin Luther King, et cetera. Finally, the attack on Wallace, which belongs in the same category.*

*   *   *

ARENDT: I think that Watergate has revealed perhaps one of the deepest constitutional crises this country has ever known. And if I say constitutional crisis, this is of course much more important than if I said *"une crise constitutionelle" en France.* For the Constitution ... I don't know how many constitutions you have had since the French Revolution. As far as I remember, by the time of World War I, you had had fourteen.

* The reference is to the May 15, 1972, assassination attempt on Alabama Governor George Wallace, who was at the time one of the front-runners in the Democratic presidential primary race.

And how many you then had . . . I don't want to tackle it, every one of you can do it better than I. But anyhow, here there is one Constitution, and this Constitution has now lasted for not quite two hundred years. Here, it's a different story. Here, it's the whole fabric of government which actually is at stake.

And this constitutional crisis consists—for the first time in the United States—in a head-on clash between the legislative and the executive. Now there the Constitution itself is somehow at fault, and I would like to talk about that for a moment. The Founding Fathers never believed that tyranny could arise out of the executive office, because they did not see this office in any different light but as the executor of what the legislation had decreed—in various forms; I leave it at that. We know today that the greatest danger of tyranny is of course from the executive. But what did the Founding Fathers—if we take the spirit of the Constitution—what did they think? They thought they were freed from majority rule, and therefore it is a great mistake if you believe that what we have here is democracy, a mistake in which many Americans share. What we have here is republican rule, and the Founding Fathers were most concerned about preserving the rights of the minorities, because they believed that in a healthy body politic there must be a plurality of opinions. That what the French call "*l'union sacrée*" is precisely what one should not have, because this would already be a kind of tyranny or the consequence of a tyranny, and the tyranny could very well be . . . The tyrant could very well be a majority. Hence, the whole government is construed in such a way that even after the victory of the majority, there is always the opposition, and the opposition is necessary because the opposition represents the legitimate opinions of either one minority or of minorities.

National security is a new word in the American vocabulary, and this, I think, you should know. National security is really, if I may already interpret a bit, a translation of *"raison d'état."* And *"raison d'état,"* this whole notion of reason of state, never played any role in this country. This is a new import. National security now covers everything, and it covers, as you may know from the interrogation of Mr. Ehrlichman,* all kinds of crimes. For instance, the president has a perfect right ... the king can do no wrong; that is, he is like a monarch in a republic. He's above the law, and his justification is always that whatever he does, he does for the sake of national security.

ERRERA: In your view, in what way are these implications of *raison d'état*, what you call the intrusion of criminality into the political domain, specific to our time? Is this, indeed, specific to our time?

ARENDT: This is *propre à notre époque* ... I really think so. Just as the stateless business is *propre à notre époque*, and repeats itself again and again under different aspects and in different countries and in different colors. But if we come to these general questions, what is also *propre à notre époque* is the massive intrusion of criminality into political processes. And by

* Arendt is alluding to the testimony of John D. Ehrlichman, President Nixon's adviser on domestic affairs, before the Senate Watergate Committee.

this I mean something which by far transcends those crimes always justified, rightly or wrongly, by *raison d'état*, because these are always the exceptions to the rule, whereas here we are confronted suddenly with a style of politics which by itself is criminal.

Here it's by no means the exception to the rule. It is not that they say, because we are in such a special emergency, we have to bug everybody and sundry, including the president himself. But they think that bugging belongs to the normal political process. And similarly, they don't say, we will burglar once, break in the office of the psychiatrist once* and then never again, by no means. They say, this is absolutely legitimate, to break in.

So this whole business of national security comes of course from the reason-of-state business. The national-security business is a direct European import. Of course, the Germans and the French and the Italians recognize it as entirely justified, because they have always lived under this. But this was precisely the European heritage with which the American Revolution intended to break.

*   *   *

ERRERA: In your essay on the Pentagon Papers† you describe the psychology of those you call the "professional

---

* The reference is to the burglary of psychiatrist Dr. Lewis Fielding's office by a covert White House special investigations unit, referred to as "the plumbers," who hoped to find material to discredit Daniel Ellsberg, the former military analyst who had leaked the Pentagon Papers.
† "Lying in Politics: Reflections on the Pentagon Papers," *New York Review of Books*, November 18, 1971, 30–39.

problem-solvers," who at the time were the advisers to the American government, and you say: "Their distinction lies in that they were problem-solvers as well, hence they were not just intelligent but prided themselves on being 'rational,' and they were indeed to a rather frightening degree above 'sentimentality' and in love with 'theory,' the world of sheer mental effort . . ."

ARENDT: May I interrupt you here? I think that's enough. I have a very good example, precisely from these Pentagon Papers, of this scientific mentality, which finally overwhelms all other insights. You know about the "domino theory," which was the official theory throughout the Cold War from 1950 till about 1969, shortly after the Pentagon Papers. The fact is that very few of the very sophisticated intellectuals who wrote the Pentagon Papers believed in this theory. There are only, I think, two or three guys, pretty high up in the administration, but not exactly very intelligent ones—Mr. Rostow and General Taylor* (not the most intelligent boy . . .)—who really believed it. That is, they didn't believe in it, but in everything they did they acted on this assumption. And this not because they were liars, or because they wanted to please their superiors—these people really were all right in this respect—but because this gave them a framework within which they could work. And they took this framework even though they

---

* Walt Whitman Rostow, who served as special assistant for National Security Affairs to Lyndon Johnson from 1964 to 1968, and General Maxwell D. Taylor, chairman of the Joint Chiefs of Staff under Kennedy from 1962 to 1964 and ambassador to South Vietnam for a year thereafter.

knew—and every intelligence report and every factual analysis proved it to them every morning—that these assumptions
were simply factually wrong. They took it because they didn't
have any other framework.

* * *

ERRERA: Our century seems to me to be dominated by the
persistence of a mode of thinking based on historical de-
terminism.

ARENDT: Yes, and I think there are very good reasons for this
belief in historical necessity. The trouble with this whole business, and it is really an open question, is the following: We
don't know the future, everybody acts into the future, and
nobody knows what he is doing, because the future is being
done. Action is a "we" and not an "I." Only where I am the
only one, if I were the only one, could I foretell what's going
to happen, from what I am doing. Now this makes it look
as though what actually happens is entirely contingent, and
contingency is indeed one of the biggest factors in all history. Nobody knows what is going to happen simply because
so much depends on an enormous amount of variables; in
other words, on simple *hasard*. On the other hand, if you look
back on history retrospectively, then you can—even though
all this was contingent—you can tell a story that makes
sense. How is that possible? That is a real problem for every
philosophy of history. How is it possible that in retrospect
it always looks as though it couldn't have happened otherwise? All the variables have disappeared, and reality has

such an overwhelming impact upon us that we cannot be bothered with what is actually an infinite variety of possibilities.

ERRERA: But if our contemporaries cling fast to determinist ways of thinking, in spite of this being refuted by history, do you think it's because they're afraid of freedom?

ARENDT: *Ja.* Sure. And rightly so. Only they don't say it. If they did, one could immediately start a debate. If they would only say it. They are afraid, they are afraid to be afraid. That is one of the main personal motivations. They are afraid of freedom.

ERRERA: Can you imagine a minister in Europe, seeing his policy about to fail, commissioning a team of experts from outside the government to produce a study whose aim would be to find out how ...

ARENDT: It was not *extérieur de l'administration.* They were taken from everywhere and also from ...

ERRERA: True, but people from outside the government were involved too. So can you imagine a European minister in the same situation commissioning a study of that kind to find out how it all happened?

ARENDT: Of course not.

ERRERA: Why not?

ARENDT: Because of reason of state, you know. He would have felt that . . . He would have immediately started to cover up. The McNamara attitude—you know, I quoted this . . .* McNamara said "It's not a very nice picture, what we are doing there; what the hell is going on here?" This is an American attitude. This shows you that things were still all right, even if they went wrong. But they were still all right because there was still McNamara who wanted to learn from it.

ERRERA: Do you think that, at present, American leaders faced with other situations still want to know?

ARENDT: No. I don't think that a single one is left. I don't know. No. No, I take that back. But I don't believe that . . . I think that McNamara was on Nixon's list of enemies, if I am not mistaken. I saw it today in *The New York Times*. I think that is true. And this shows you already that this whole attitude has gone out of American politics—that is, on the highest level. It is no longer there. They believed, you see, these people already believed in image-making, but still with a vengeance, that is: Why didn't we succeed with image-making? And one can say that it was only images, you know. But now they want everybody to believe in their images, and nobody should look beyond them, and that is of course an altogether different political will.

* Arendt is referring to the epigraph she chose for "Lying in Politics," which was the following quote from Robert S. McNamara: "The picture of the world's greatest superpower killing or seriously injuring a thousand non-combatants a week, while trying to pound a tiny backward nation into submission on an issue whose merits are hotly disputed, is not a pretty one."

ERRERA: After what Senator Fulbright calls the "arrogance of power,"* after what we might call the "arrogance of knowledge," is there a third stage that is arrogance pure and simple?

ARENDT: Yes, I don't know whether it's *l'arrogance tout court.* It is really the will to dominate, for heaven's sake. And up to now it hasn't succeeded, because I still sit with you at this table and talk pretty freely. So they haven't yet dominated me; and somehow I am not afraid. Perhaps I am mistaken, but I feel perfectly free in this country. So they haven't succeeded. Somebody, I think Morgenthau,[†] called this whole Nixon enterprise an "abortive revolution." Now, we don't yet know whether it was abortive—it was early when he said that—but there's one thing one can say: successful it wasn't either.

* * *

ERRERA: But isn't the big threat these days the idea that the goals of politics are limitless? Liberalism, after all, presupposes the idea that politics has limited objectives. These days, doesn't the biggest threat come from the rise of men and movements who set themselves unlimited objectives?

ARENDT: I hope I don't shock you if I tell you that I'm not at all sure that I'm a liberal. You know, not at all. And I really

---

* Errera is referring to the concept that Arkansas Senator James Fulbright laid out in his 1966 book *The Arrogance of Power*, in which he took the U.S. government to task for the justifications it had offered for the Vietnam War.
† Hans Morgenthau, an influential scholar of international relations and foreign policy, and author of *Politics Among Nations*.

don't have any creed in this sense. I have no exact political philosophy which I could summon up with one ism.

ERRERA: Of course, but all the same your philosophical reflections lie within the foundations of liberal thought, with its borrowings from antiquity.

ARENDT: Is Montesquieu a liberal? Would you say that all the people whom I take into account as worth a little ... I mean, *"moi je me sers où je peux"* [I help myself to what I can]. I take whatever I can and whatever suits me. I think one of the great advantages of our time is really, you know, what René Char has said: *"Notre héritage n'est garanti par aucun testament"* [Our inheritance is guaranteed by no testament].*

ERRERA: ... is preceded by no testament ...

ARENDT: ... *n'est précédé par aucun testament.* This means we are entirely free to help ourselves wherever we can from the experiences and the thoughts of our past.

ERRERA: But doesn't this extreme freedom risk alarming many of our contemporaries who would prefer to find some ready-made theory, some ideology they could then apply?

---

* The correct quotation from Char is *"Notre héritage n'est précédé d'aucun testament,*" which is taken from *Feuillets d'Hypnos* (Paris: Gallimard, 1946). Arendt uses this quotation as the opening words of *Between Past and Future: Eight Exercises in Political Thought* (New York: Viking, 1968), where she translates it as "Our inheritance was left to us by no testament."

ARENDT: *Certainement. Aucun doute. Aucun doute.*

ERRERA: Doesn't this freedom risk being the freedom of a few, those who are strong enough to invent new modes of thought?

ARENDT: *Non. Non.* It rests only on the conviction that every human being is a thinking being and can reflect as well as I do and can therefore judge for himself, if he wants to. How I can make this wish arise in him, this I don't know. The only thing that can help us, I think, is to *réfléchir.* And to think always means to think critically. And to think critically is always to be hostile. Every thought actually undermines whatever there is of rigid rules, general convictions, et cetera. Everything which happens in thinking is subject to a critical examination of whatever there is. That is, there are no dangerous thoughts for the simple reason that thinking itself is such a dangerous enterprise. So how I can convince . . . I think, nonthinking is even more dangerous. I don't deny that thinking is dangerous, but I would say not thinking, *ne pas réfléchir c'est plus dangereux encore* [not thinking is even more dangerous].

ERRERA: Let's go back to René Char's words: "Our inheritance is preceded by no testament." What do you think the inheritance of the twentieth century will be?

ARENDT: We are still there, you know—you are young, I am old—but we are both still there to leave them something.

ERRERA: What will we leave to the twenty-first century? Three quarters of the century have already gone by ...

ARENDT: I've no idea. I'm pretty sure that modern art which is now rather at a deep point ... But after such an enormous creativity as we had during the first forty years, especially in France, of course, this is only natural. A certain exhaustion then sets in. This we will leave. This whole era, this whole twentieth century will probably be one of the great centuries in history, but not in politics.

ERRERA: And America?

ARENDT: No. No, no, no ...

ERRERA: Why?

ARENDT: You know, this country ... You need a certain amount of tradition.

ERRERA: There isn't an American artistic tradition?

ARENDT: No, not a great one. A great one in poetry, a great one in novels, in writing, et cetera. But the only thing that you could really mention is this, the architecture. The stone buildings are like tents of nomads which have been frozen into stone.

*   *   *

ERRERA: In your work, you've frequently discussed the

modern history of the Jews and anti-Semitism, and you say, at the end of one of your books, that the birth of the Zionist movement at the end of the nineteenth century was the only political response the Jews ever found to anti-Semitism.* In what way has the existence of Israel changed the political and psychological context in which Jews live in the world?

ARENDT: Oh, I think it has changed everything. The Jewish people today are really united behind Israel.† They feel that they have a state, a political representation in the same way as the Irish, the English, the French, et cetera. They have not only a homeland but a nation-state. And their whole attitude towards the Arabs depends, of course, to a large extent on these identifications, which the Jews coming from Central Europe made almost instinctively and without reflection; namely, that the state must necessarily be a nation-state.

Now this, that is, the whole relationship between the Diaspora and Israel, or what formerly was Palestine, has changed because Israel is no longer just a refuge for those underdogs in Poland, where a Zionist was a guy who tried to get money from rich Jews for the poor Jews in Poland. But it is today really the Jewish representative of the Jewish people all over the world. Whether we like that or not is another question,

---

* *The Origins of Totalitarianism* (New York: Harcourt, Brace & World, 1951), 155.
† This should be read against the background of the events of the day: on October 6, 1973, Egypt and Syria had attacked Israel, unleashing the Yom Kippur War.

but ... This doesn't mean that this Diaspora Judaism has to always be of the same opinion as the government in Israel. It's not a question of the government, it's a question of the state and so long as the state exists, this is of course what represents us in the eyes of the world.

ERRERA: Ten years ago, a French author, Georges Friedmann, wrote a book called *The End of the Jewish People?,** in which he concluded that in the future there would be, on the one hand, a new state, an Israeli nation, and on the other, in the lands of the Diaspora, Jews who would be assimilated and would gradually lose their own characteristics.

ARENDT: *Cette hypothèse* sounds very plausible, and I think it's quite wrong. You see, in antiquity, while the Jewish state still existed, there was already a great Jewish Diaspora. Through the centuries, when there were many different forms of government and forms of state, the Jews, the only ancient people that actually survived these thousands of years, were never assimilated ... If Jews could have been assimilated, they would have been assimilated long ago. There was a chance during the Spanish period, there was a chance during the Roman period, there was, of course, a chance in the eighteenth and nineteenth centuries. Look, a people, a collective, doesn't commit suicide. Mr. Friedmann is wrong, because he doesn't understand that the feeling of the intellectuals, who can indeed change nationalities and can absorb another culture, et cetera, does not correspond to the feeling of the people as a whole,

* Georges Friedmann, *Fin du peuple juif?* (Paris: Gallimard, 1965).

and especially not of a people that has been constituted by those laws which we all know.

ERRERA: What does it mean for Jews to be assimilated into American society?

ARENDT: Well, in the sense in which we spoke of assimilated Jewry, by which we meant assimilation to the surrounding culture, it doesn't exist. Would you kindly tell me to what the Jews should assimilate here? To the English? To the Irish? To the Germans? To the French? To the ... you know, whoever came here ...

ERRERA: When people say that American Jews are very Americanized, not just Americans but Americanized, what are they getting at?

ARENDT: One means the way of life, and all these Jews are very good American citizens ... That is, it signifies their public life, not their private life, not their social life. And their social and their private life is today more Jewish than it ever was before. The younger generation in great numbers learn Hebrew, even if they are from parents who don't know any Hebrew any longer. But the main thing is really Israel, the main thing is: Are you for or against Israel?

Take, for example, the German Jews of my generation who came to this country. They became in no time at all very nationalistic Jews, much more nationalistic than I ever was, even though I was a Zionist and they were not. I never said I'm a German, I always said I'm a Jew. But they now assimilate.

To what? To the Jewish community, since they were used to assimilation. They assimilated to the Jewish community of America and that means that they then of course, with the fervor of new converts, became especially nationalistic and pro-Israel.

ERRERA: Throughout history, what has ensured the survival of the Jewish people has been, mainly, a religious kind of bond. We are living in a period when religions as a whole are going through a crisis, where people are trying to loosen the shackles of religion. In these conditions, what, in the current period, comprises the unity of the Jewish people throughout the world?

ARENDT: I think you are slightly wrong with this thesis. When you say religion, you think, of course, of the Christian religion, which is a creed and a faith. This is not at all true for the Jewish religion. This is really a national religion where nation and religion coincide. You know that Jews, for instance, don't recognize baptism and for them it is as though it hadn't happened. That is, a Jew never ceases to be a Jew according to Jewish law. So long as somebody is born by a Jewish mother—*la recherche de la paternité est interdite* [he is forbidden from trying to find out who his father was]—he is a Jew. The notion of what religion is, is altogether different. It's much more a way of life than it is a religion in the particular, specific sense of the Christian religion. I remember, for instance, I had Jewish instruction, religious instruction, and when I was about fourteen years old, of course I wanted to rebel and do something terrible to our teacher and I got up and said "I don't believe in God." Whereupon he said: "Who asked you?"

* * *

ERRERA: Your first book, published in 1951, was called *The Origins of Totalitarianism*. In this book you tried not just to describe a phenomenon but also to explain it. Hence this question: In your view, what is totalitarianism?

ARENDT: *Oui, enfin* . . . Let me start with making certain distinctions upon which other people . . . They are not agreed upon. First of all, a totalitarian dictatorship is neither a simple dictatorship nor a simple tyranny.

When I analyzed a totalitarian government, I tried to analyze it as a new form of government that wasn't known before, and therefore I tried to enumerate its main characteristics. Among these, I would just like to remind you of one characteristic which is entirely absent from all tyrannies today, and that is the role of the innocent, the innocent victim. Under Stalin you didn't have to do anything in order to be deported or in order to be killed. You were given the role according to the dynamism of history and you had to play this role no matter what you did. With respect to this, no government before has killed people for saying yes. Usually a government kills people or tyrants kill people for saying no. Now, I was reminded by a friend that something very similar was said in China many centuries ago, namely that men who have the impertinence to approve are no better than the

disobedient who oppose. And this of course is the quintessen-
tial sign of totalitarianism, in that there is a total domination
of men by men.

Now, in this sense there is no totalitarianism today, even
in Russia, which has one of the worst tyrannies we have ever
known. Even in Russia you have to do something in order to
be sent away into exile, or a forced labor camp, or a psychiat-
ric ward of a hospital.

Now, let's for a moment see what tyranny is, because
after all totalitarian regimes arose when the majority of European governments were already under dictatorships. Dictatorships, if we take them in the original sense of the concept,
of the word, are not tyrannies; there's a temporary suspension
of the laws in the case of an emergency, usually during a war
or civil war or such. But, anyhow, the dictatorship is limited
in time and tyranny is not . . .

* * *

ARENDT: When I wrote my *Eichmann in Jerusalem*, one of my
main intentions was to destroy the legend of the greatness of
evil, of the demonic force, to take away from people the ad-
miration they have for the great evildoers like Richard III or
et cetera. I found in Brecht* the following remark: "The great
political criminals must be exposed and exposed especially to
laughter. They are not great political criminals, but people who

_____

* This quotation is taken from Brecht's notes to the play "The Resistible
Rise of Arturo Ui" in *Werke: Große kommentierte Berliner und Frankfurter Ausgabe* (Berlin: Suhrkamp, 1988), 24:315–19.

permitted great political crimes, which is something entirely different. The failure of his enterprises does not indicate that Hitler was an idiot." Now, that Hitler was an idiot was, of course, a prejudice of all—of the whole opposition to Hitler prior to his seizure of power. And therefore a great many books tried to justify him and to make him a great man. So he [Brecht] says: "That he failed did not indicate that Hitler was an idiot and the extent of his enterprises does not make him a great man." That is, neither the one nor the other; this whole category of greatness has no application. "If the ruling classes," says he, "permit a small crook to become a great crook, he is not entitled to a privileged position in our view of history. That is, the fact that he becomes a great crook and that what he does has great consequences does not add to his stature." And generally speaking, he [Brecht] then says in these rather abrupt remarks: "One may state that tragedy deals with the sufferings of mankind in a less serious way than comedy."

This, of course, is a shocking statement. I think that at the same time it is entirely true. What is really necessary is—if you want to keep your integrity under these circumstances—then you can do it only if you remember your old way of looking at such things and say: No matter what he does, if he killed ten million people, he is still a clown.

ERRERA: When you published your book on the Eichmann trial, it aroused some very violent reactions. Why were there such reactions?

ARENDT: Well, as I said before, this controversy was partly caused by the fact that I attacked the bureaucracy, and if you attack a bureaucracy, you have got to be prepared for the fact that this bureaucracy will defend itself, will attack you, will try to make you impossible and everything which goes with it. That is, more or less, dirty political business. Now, with this I really had no real quarrel. But suppose they had not done it, suppose they had not organized this campaign, then still the opposition to this book would have been strong, because the Jewish people were offended, and now I mean people whom I really respect. And therefore I can understand it. They were offended chiefly by what Brecht referred to, by laughter. My laughter was, at that time, kind of innocent and kind of not reflecting on my laughter. What I saw was a clown.

So, Eichmann, for instance, was bothered never by anything which he had done to the Jews in general. But he was bothered by one little incident: he had slapped the face of the then president of the Jewish community in Vienna during an interrogation. God knows many worse things were happening to many people than to be slapped in the face. But this he has never condoned himself for having done, and he thought this was very wrong, indeed. He had lost his cool, so to speak.

*   *   *

ERRERA: Why do you think we are seeing the emergence of a whole literature that, when it comes to Nazism, for instance, often describes its leaders and their crimes in a novelistic way and tries to humanize them, and thereby indirectly to justify them? Do you think that publications of this kind are purely commercial, or do they have a deeper significance?

ARENDT: I think it has a *signification*, at least it shows that what happened once can happen again, and this indeed, I believe, is entirely true. You see, tyranny has been discovered very early, and identified very early as an enemy. Still, it has never in any way prevented any tyrant from becoming a tyrant. It has not prevented Nero, and it has not prevented Caligula. And the cases of Nero and Caligula have not prevented an even closer example of what the massive intrusion of criminality can mean for the political process.

HANNAH ARENDT (1906–1975) was a political theorist and scholar. Born in Germany into a family of secular Jews, as a young woman she studied philosophy with Martin Heidegger and Karl Jaspers. In 1933, she was arrested and interrogated by the Gestapo, and subsequently interned in a concentration camp in the south of France, Camp Gurs. She fled to the United States in 1941 with her husband Heinrich Blücher. In the United States, she served as a visiting scholar at the University of California, Berkeley, the University of Chicago, Northwestern, Wesleyan, Princeton, Yale, and the New School for Social Research. She died in New York City at the age of sixty-nine.

ANDREW BROWN is a Cambridge-based translator from French and German, and the author of *Roland Barthes: The Figures of Writing*.

ROGER ERRERA is a former member of the *Conseil d'Etat*, France's Supreme Court for administrative law, and the United Nations Human Rights Committee, and an Honorary Fellow of the University of London. He is the author of a number of essays on media law, judicial institutions, immigration and refugee law, and European law. His most recent book is an essay on justice in France, *Et ce sera justice . . . : Le juge dans la cité* (Paris: Gallimard, 2013).

JOACHIM FEST (1926–2006) was a historian, journalist, and critic. He was the son of strongly anti-Nazi parents who refused to enroll him in the Hitler Youth. He edited the cultural section of the *Frankfurter Allgemeine Zeitung* from 1973 to 1993. He is also the author of a major biography of Hitler and other works on the Third Reich, including *Inside Hitler's Bunker: The Last Days of the Third Reich*, *Speer: The Final Verdict*, and *Plotting Hitler's Death: The German Resistance to Hitler, 1933–1945*.

GÜNTER GAUS (1929–2004) was a journalist, television presenter, and politician. His show, *Zur Person* (In person), in which he interviewed politicians, scientists, and artists, ran from 1963 to 2003.

DENVER LINDLEY was an editor at Henry Holt, Harcourt Brace, and the Viking Press. His translations include Thomas Mann's *Confessions of Felix Krull, Confidence Man: The Early Years*, Erich Maria Remarque's *Arch of Triumph*, and André Maurois's *Memoirs: 1885–1967*.

URSULA LUDZ is the editor of *Letters: 1925–1975 by Hannah Arendt and Martin Heidegger, Denktagebuch* (together with Ingeborg Nordmann) and *Ich will verstehen*, a collection of autobiographical statements by Arendt and a complete bibliography of her works. She is also a member of the editorial staff of the Internet journal HannahArendt.net.

ADELBERT REIF is a journalist and the editor of Claude Lévi-Strauss's *Myth and Meaning: Five Radio Talks*, among other books.

JOAN STAMBAUGH is Professor Emeritus at Hunter College, and the translator of a number of books by Martin Heidegger, including *Being and Time, Identity and Difference*, and *The End of Philosophy*.

THE LAST INTERVIEW SERIES

KURT VONNEGUT: THE LAST INTERVIEW

"I think it can be tremendously refreshing if a creator of literature has something on his mind other than the history of literature so far. Literature should not disappear up its own asshole, so to speak."

$15.95 / $17.95 CAN
978-1-61219-090-7
ebook: 978-1-61219-091-4

LEARNING TO LIVE FINALLY: THE LAST INTERVIEW
JACQUES DERRIDA

"I am at war with myself, it's true, you couldn't possibly know to what extent . . . I say contradictory things that are, we might say, in real tension; they are what construct me, make me live, and will make me die."

translated by PASCAL-ANNE BRAULT and MICHAEL NAAS

$15.95 / $17.95 CAN
978-1-61219-094-5
ebook: 978-1-61219-032-7

ROBERTO BOLAÑO: THE LAST INTERVIEW

"Posthumous: It sounds like the name of a Roman gladiator, an unconquered gladiator. At least that's what poor Posthumous would like to believe. It gives him courage."

translated by SYBIL PEREZ and others

$15.95 / $17.95 CAN
978-1-61219-095-2
ebook: 978-1-61219-033-4

THE LAST INTERVIEW SERIES

DAVID FOSTER WALLACE: THE LAST INTERVIEW

"I don't know what you're thinking or what it's like inside you and you don't know what it's like inside me. In fiction... we can leap over that wall itself in a certain way."

$15.95 / $15.95 CAN
978-1-61219-206-2
ebook: 978-1-61219-207-9

JORGE LUIS BORGES: THE LAST INTERVIEW

"Believe me: the benefits of blindness have been greatly exaggerated. If I could see, I would never leave the house, I'd stay indoors reading the many books that surround me."

translated by KIT MAUDE

$15.95 / $15.95 CAN
978-1-61219-204-8
ebook: 978-1-61219-205-5

HANNAH ARENDT: THE LAST INTERVIEW

"There are no dangerous thoughts for the simple reason that thinking itself is such a dangerous enterprise."

$15.95 / $15.95 CAN
978-1-61219-311-3
ebook: 978-1-61219-312-0